Memoir of Fleeming Jenkin

R. L. Stevenson

Memoir of Fleeming Jenkin
Robert Louis Stevenson

© 1st World Library – Literary Society, 2004
PO Box 2211
Fairfield, IA 52556
www.1stworldlibrary.org
First Edition

LCCN: 2003195135

ISBN: 1-59540-508-9

Purchase *"Memoir of Fleeming Jenkin"*
as a traditional bound book at:
www.1stWorldLibrary.org/purchase.asp?ISBN=1-59540-508-9

1st World Library Literary Society is a nonprofit organization dedicated to promoting literacy by:

- Creating a free internet library accessible from any computer worldwide.
- Hosting writing competitions and offering book publishing scholarships.

Readers interested in supporting literacy
through sponsorship, donations or
membership please contact:
literacy@1stworldlibrary.org
Check us out at: www.1stworldlibrary.org

Memoir of Fleeming Jenkin
*contributed by the Charles Family
in support of
1st World Library - Literary Society*

PREFACE TO THE AMERICAN EDITION.

ON the death of Fleeming Jenkin, his family and friends determined to publish a selection of his various papers; by way of introduction, the following pages were drawn up; and the whole, forming two considerable volumes, has been issued in England. In the States, it has not been thought advisable to reproduce the whole; and the memoir appearing alone, shorn of that other matter which was at once its occasion and its justification, so large an account of a man so little known may seem to a stranger out of all proportion. But Jenkin was a man much more remarkable than the mere bulk or merit of his work approves him. It was in the world, in the commerce of friendship, by his brave attitude towards life, by his high moral value and unwearied intellectual effort, that he struck the minds of his contemporaries. His was an individual figure, such as authors delight to draw, and all men to read of, in the pages of a novel. His was a face worth painting for its own sake. If the sitter shall not seem to have justified the portrait, if Jenkin, after his death, shall not continue to make new friends, the fault will be altogether mine.

R. L S.

SARANAC, OCT., 1887.

CHAPTER I.

The Jenkins of Stowting - Fleeming's grandfather - Mrs. Buckner's fortune - Fleeming's father; goes to sea; at St. Helena; meets King Tom; service in the West Indies; end of his career - The Campbell-Jacksons - Fleeming's mother - Fleeming's uncle John.

IN the reign of Henry VIII., a family of the name of Jenkin, claiming to come from York, and bearing the arms of Jenkin ap Philip of St. Melans, are found reputably settled in the county of Kent. Persons of strong genealogical pinion pass from William Jenkin, Mayor of Folkestone in 1555, to his contemporary 'John Jenkin, of the Citie of York, Receiver General of the County,' and thence, by way of Jenkin ap Philip, to the proper summit of any Cambrian pedigree - a prince; 'Guaith Voeth, Lord of Cardigan,' the name and style of him. It may suffice, however, for the present, that these Kentish Jenkins must have undoubtedly derived from Wales, and being a stock of some efficiency, they struck roct and grew to wealth and consequence in their new home.

Of their consequence we have proof enough in the fact that not only was William Jenkin (as already mentioned) Mayor of Folkestone in 1555, but no less than twenty-three times in the succeeding century and a half, a Jenkin (William, Thomas, Henry, or Robert) sat in the same place of humble honour. Of their wealth we know that in the reign of Charles I., Thomas Jenkin of Eythorne was more than once in the market buying land, and notably, in 1633, acquired the manor of Stowting Court. This was an estate of some 320 acres, six miles from Hythe, in the Bailiwick and Hundred of Stowting, and the Lathe of Shipway, held of the Crown IN CAPITE by the service of six men and a constable to defend the passage of the sea at Sandgate. It had a chequered history before it fell into the hands of Thomas of Eythorne, having been sold and given from one to another - to the Archbishop, to Heringods, to the Burghershes, to Pavelys, Trivets, Cliffords, Wenlocks, Beauchamps, Nevilles, Kempes, and Clarkes: a piece of Kentish ground condemned to see new faces and to be no man's home. But from 1633 onward it became the anchor of the Jenkin family in Kent; and though passed on from brother to brother, held in shares between uncle and nephew, burthened by debts and jointures, and at least once sold and bought in again, it remains to this day in the hands of the direct line. It is not my design, nor have I the necessary knowledge, to give a history of this obscure family. But this is an age when genealogy has taken a new lease of life, and become for the first time a human science; so that we no longer study it in quest of the Guaith Voeths, but to trace out some of the secrets of descent and destiny; and as we study, we think less of Sir Bernard Burke and more of Mr. Galton. Not only do our character and talents lie upon the anvil and receive their temper during generations; but the very plot of our life's story unfolds itself on a scale of centuries, and the biography of the man is only an episode in the epic of the family. From this point of view I ask the reader's leave to begin this notice of a remarkable man who was my friend, with the accession of his great-grandfather, John Jenkin.

This John Jenkin, a grandson of Damaris Kingsley, of the family of 'Westward Ho!' was born in 1727, and married Elizabeth, daughter of Thomas Frewen, of Church House, Northiam. The Jenkins had now been long enough intermarrying with their Kentish neighbours to be Kentish folk themselves in all but name; and with the Frewens in particular their connection is singularly involved. John and his wife were each descended in the third degree from another Thomas Frewen, Vicar of Northiam, and brother to Accepted Frewen, Archbishop of York. John's mother had married a Frewen for a second husband. And the last complication was to be added by the Bishop of Chichester's brother, Charles Buckner, Vice-Admiral of the White, who was twice married, first to a paternal cousin of Squire John, and second to Anne, only sister of the Squire's wife, and already the widow of another Frewen. The reader must bear Mrs. Buckner in mind; it was by means of that lady that Fleeming Jenkin began life as a poor man. Meanwhile, the relationship of any Frewen to any Jenkin at the end of these evolutions presents a problem almost insoluble; and we need not wonder if Mrs. John, thus exercised in her immediate circle, was in her old age 'a great genealogist of all Sussex families, and much consulted.' The names Frewen and Jenkin may almost seem to have been interchangeable at will; and yet Fate proceeds with such particularity that it was perhaps on the point of name that the family was ruined.

The John Jenkins had a family of one daughter and five extravagant and unpractical sons. The eldest, Stephen, entered the Church and held the living of Salehurst, where he offered, we may hope, an extreme example of the clergy of the age. He was a handsome figure of a man; jovial and jocular; fond of his garden, which produced under his care the finest fruits of the neighbourhood; and like all the family, very choice in horses. He drove tandem; like Jehu, furiously. His saddle horse, Captain (for the names of horses are piously preserved in the family chronicle which I follow), was trained to break into a gallop as soon as the vicar's foot was thrown across its back; nor would the rein be drawn in the nine miles between Northiam and the Vicarage door. Debt was the man's proper element; he used to skulk from arrest in the chancel of his church; and the speed of Captain may have come sometimes handy. At an early age this unconventional parson married his cook, and by her he had two daughters and one son. One of the daughters died unmarried; the other imitated her father, and married 'imprudently.' The son, still more gallantly continuing the tradition, entered the army, loaded himself with debt, was forced to sell out, took refuge in the Marines, and was lost on the Dogger Bank in the war-ship MINOTAUR. If he did not marry below him, like his father, his sister, and a certain great-uncle William, it was perhaps because he never married at all.

The second brother, Thomas, who was employed in the General Post-Office, followed in all material points the example of Stephen, married 'not very creditably,' and spent all the money he could lay his hands on. He died without issue; as did the fourth brother, John, who was of weak intellect and feeble health, and the fifth brother, William, whose brief career as one of Mrs. Buckner's satellites will fall to be considered later on. So soon, then, as the MINOTAUR had struck upon the Dogger Bank, Stowting and the line of the Jenkin family fell on the shoulders of the third brother, Charles.

Facility and self-indulgence are the family marks; facility (to judge by these imprudent marriages) being at once their quality and their defect; but in the case of Charles, a man of exceptional beauty and sweetness both of face and disposition, the family fault had quite grown to be a virtue, and we find him in consequence the drudge and milk-cow of his relatives. Born in 1766, Charles served at sea in his youth, and smelt both salt water and powder. The Jenkins had inclined hitherto, as far as I can make out, to the land service. Stephen's son had been a soldier; William (fourth of Stowting) had been an officer of the unhappy Braddock's in America, where, by the way, he owned and afterwards sold an estate on the James River, called, after the parental seat; of which I should like well to hear if it still bears the name. It was probably by the influence of Captain Buckner, already connected with the family by his first marriage, that Charles Jenkin turned his mind in the direction of the navy; and it was in Buckner's own ship, the PROTHEE, 64, that the lad made his only campaign. It was in the days of Rodney's war, when the PROTHEE, we read, captured two large privateers to windward of Barbadoes, and was 'materially and distinguishedly engaged' in both the actions with De Grasse. While at sea Charles kept a journal, and made strange archaic pilot-book sketches, part plan, part elevation, some of which survive for the amusement of posterity. He did a good deal of surveying, so that here we may perhaps lay our finger on the beginning of Fleeming's education as an engineer. What is still more strange, among the relics of the handsome midshipman and his stay in the gun-room of the PROTHEE, I find a code of signals graphically represented, for all the world as it would have been done by his grandson.

On the declaration of peace, Charles, because he had suffered from scurvy, received his mother's orders to retire; and he was not the man to refuse a request, far less to disobey a command. Thereupon he turned farmer, a trade he was to practice on a large scale; and we find him married to a Miss Schirr, a woman of some fortune, the daughter of a London merchant. Stephen, the not very reverend, was still alive, galloping about the country or skulking in his chancel. It does not appear whether he let or sold the paternal manor to Charles; one or other, it must have been; and the sailor-farmer settled at Stowting, with his wife, his mother, his unmarried sister, and his sick brother John. Out of the six people of whom his nearest family consisted, three were in his own house, and two others (the horse-leeches, Stephen and Thomas) he appears to have continued to assist with more amiability than wisdom. He hunted, belonged to the Yeomanry, owned famous horses, Maggie and Lucy, the latter coveted by royalty itself. 'Lord Rokeby, his neighbour, called him kinsman,' writes my artless chronicler, 'and altogether life was very cheery.' At Stowting his three sons, John, Charles, and Thomas Frewen, and his younger daughter, Anna, were all born to him; and the reader should here be told that it is through the report of this second Charles (born 1801) that he has been looking on at these confused passages of family history.

In the year 1805 the ruin of the Jenkins was begun. It was the work of a fallacious lady already mentioned, Aunt Anne Frewen, a sister of Mrs. John. Twice married, first to her cousin Charles Frewen, clerk to the Court of Chancery, Brunswick Herald, and Usher of the Black Rod, and secondly to Admiral Buckner, she was denied issue in both beds, and being very rich - she died worth about 60,000L., mostly in land - she was in perpetual quest of an heir. The mirage of this fortune hung before successive members of the Jenkin family until her death in 1825, when it dissolved and left the latest Alnaschar face to face with bankruptcy. The grandniece, Stephen's daughter, the one who had not 'married imprudently,' appears to have been the first; for she was taken abroad by the golden aunt, and died in her care at Ghent in 1792. Next she adopted William, the youngest of the five nephews; took him abroad with her - it seems as if that were in the formula; was shut up with him in Paris by the Revolution; brought him back to Windsor, and got him a place in the King's Body-Guard, where he attracted the notice of George III. by his proficiency in German. In 1797, being on guard at St. James's Palace, William took a cold which carried him off; and Aunt Anne was once more left heirless. Lastly, in 1805, perhaps moved by the Admiral, who had a kindness for his old midshipman, perhaps pleased by the good looks and the good nature of the man himself, Mrs. Buckner turned her eyes upon Charles Jenkin. He was not only to be the heir, however, he was to be the chief hand in a somewhat wild scheme of family farming. Mrs. Jenkin, the mother, contributed 164 acres of land; Mrs. Buckner, 570, some at Northiam, some farther off; Charles let one-half of Stowting to a tenant, and threw the other and various scattered parcels into the common enterprise; so that the whole farm amounted to near upon a thousand acres, and was scattered over thirty miles of country. The ex-seaman of thirty-nine, on whose wisdom and ubiquity the scheme depended, was to live in the meanwhile without care or fear. He was to check himself in nothing; his two extravagances, valuable horses and worthless brothers, were to be indulged in comfort; and whether the year quite paid itself or not, whether successive years left accumulated savings or only a growing deficit, the fortune of the golden aunt should in the end repair all.

On this understanding Charles Jenkin transported his family to Church House, Northiam: Charles the second, then a child of three, among the number. Through the eyes of the boy we have glimpses of the life that followed: of Admiral and Mrs. Buckner driving up from Windsor in a coach and six, two post-horses and their own four; of the house full of visitors, the great roasts at the fire, the tables in the servants' hall laid for thirty or forty for a month together; of the daily press of neighbours, many of whom, Frewens, Lords, Bishops, Batchellors, and Dynes, were also kinsfolk; and the parties 'under the great spreading chestnuts of the old fore court,' where the young people danced and made merry to the music of the village band. Or perhaps, in the depth of winter, the father would bid young Charles saddle his pony; they would ride the thirty miles from Northiam to Stowting, with the snow to the pony's saddle girths, and be received by the tenants like princes.

This life of delights, with the continual visible comings and goings of the golden aunt, was well qualified to relax the fibre of the lads. John, the heir, a yeoman and a fox-hunter, 'loud and notorious with his whip and spurs,' settled down into a kind of Tony Lumpkin, waiting for the shoes of his father and his aunt. Thomas Frewen, the youngest, is briefly dismissed as 'a handsome beau'; but he had the merit or the good fortune to become a doctor of medicine, so that when the crash came he was not empty-handed for the war of life. Charles, at the day-school of Northiam, grew so well acquainted with the rod, that his floggings became matter of pleasantry and reached the ears of Admiral

Buckner. Hereupon that tall, rough-voiced, formidable uncle entered with the lad into a covenant: every time that Charles was thrashed he was to pay the Admiral a penny; everyday that he escaped, the process was to be reversed. 'I recollect,' writes Charles, 'going crying to my mother to be taken to the Admiral to pay my debt.' It would seem by these terms the speculation was a losing one; yet it is probable it paid indirectly by bringing the boy under remark. The Admiral was no enemy to dunces; he loved courage, and Charles, while yet little more than a baby, would ride the great horse into the pond. Presently it was decided that here was the stuff of a fine sailor; and at an early period the name of Charles Jenkin was entered on a ship's books.

From Northiam he was sent to another school at Boonshill, near Rye, where the master took 'infinite delight' in strapping him. 'It keeps me warm and makes you grow,' he used to say. And the stripes were not altogether wasted, for the dunce, though still very 'raw,' made progress with his studies. It was known, moreover, that he was going to sea, always a ground of pre-eminence with schoolboys; and in his case the glory was not altogether future, it wore a present form when he came driving to Rye behind four horses in the same carriage with an admiral. 'I was not a little proud, you may believe,' says he.

In 1814, when he was thirteen years of age, he was carried by his father to Chichester to the Bishop's Palace. The Bishop had heard from his brother the Admiral that Charles was likely to do well, and had an order from Lord Melville for the lad's admission to the Royal Naval College at Portsmouth. Both the Bishop and the Admiral patted him on the head and said, 'Charles will restore the old family'; by which I gather with some surprise that, even in these days of open house at Northiam and golden hope of my aunt's fortune, the family was supposed to stand in need of restoration. But the past is apt to look brighter than nature, above all to those enamoured of their genealogy; and the ravages of Stephen and Thomas must have always given matter of alarm.

What with the flattery of bishops and admirals, the fine company in which he found himself at Portsmouth, his visits home, with their gaiety and greatness of life, his visits to Mrs. Buckner (soon a widow) at Windsor, where he had a pony kept for him, and visited at Lord Melville's and Lord Harcourt's and the Leveson-Gowers, he began to have 'bumptious notions,' and his head was 'somewhat turned with fine people'; as to some extent it remained throughout his innocent and honourable life.

In this frame of mind the boy was appointed to the CONQUEROR, Captain Davie, humorously known as Gentle Johnnie. The captain had earned this name by his style of discipline, which would have figured well in the pages of Marryat: 'Put the prisoner's head in a bag and give him another dozen!' survives as a specimen of his commands; and the men were often punished twice or thrice in a week. On board the ship of this disciplinarian, Charles and his father were carried in a billy-boat from Sheerness in December, 1816: Charles with an outfit suitable to his pretensions, a twenty-guinea sextant and 120 dollars in silver, which were ordered into the care of the gunner. 'The old clerks and mates,' he writes, 'used to laugh and jeer me for joining the ship in a billy-boat, and when they found I was from Kent, vowed I was an old Kentish smuggler. This to my pride, you will believe, was not a little offensive.'

THE CONQUEROR carried the flag of Vice-Admiral Plampin, commanding at the Cape and St. Helena; and at that all-important islet, in July, 1817, she relieved the flagship of Sir Pulteney Malcolm. Thus it befel that Charles Jenkin, coming too late for the epic of the French wars, played a small part in the dreary and disgraceful afterpiece of St. Helena. Life on the guard-ship was onerous and irksome. The anchor was never lifted, sail never made, the great guns were silent; none was allowed on shore except on duty; all day the movements of the imperial captive were signalled to and fro; all night the boats rowed guard around the accessible portions of the coast. This prolonged stagnation and petty watchfulness in what Napoleon himself called that 'unchristian' climate, told cruelly on the health of the ship's company. In eighteen months, according to O'Meara, the CONQUEROR had lost one hundred and ten men and invalided home one hundred and seven, being more than a third of her complement. It does not seem that our young midshipman so much as once set eyes on Bonaparte; and yet in other ways Jenkin was more fortunate than some of his comrades. He drew in water-colour; not so badly as his father, yet ill enough; and this art was so rare aboard the CONQUEROR that even his humble proficiency marked him out and procured him some alleviations. Admiral Plampin had succeeded Napoleon at the Briars; and here he had young Jenkin staying with him to make sketches of the historic house. One of these is before me as I write, and gives a strange notion of the arts in our old English Navy. Yet it was again as an artist that the lad was taken for a run to Rio, and apparently for a second outing in a ten-gun brig. These, and a cruise of six weeks to windward of the island undertaken by the CONQUEROR herself in quest of health, were the only breaks in three years of murderous inaction; and at the end of that period Jenkin was invalided home, having 'lost his health entirely.'

As he left the deck of the guard-ship the historic part of his career came to an end. For forty-two years he continued to serve his country obscurely on the seas, sometimes thanked for inconspicuous and honourable services, but denied any opportunity of serious distinction. He was first two years in the LARNE, Captain Tait, hunting pirates and keeping a watch on the Turkish and Greek squadrons in the Archipelago. Captain Tait was a favourite with Sir Thomas Maitland, High Commissioner of the Ionian Islands - King Tom as he was called - who frequently took passage in the LARNE. King Tom knew every inch of the Mediterranean, and was a terror to the officers of the watch. He would come on deck at night; and with his broad Scotch accent, 'Well, sir,' he would say, 'what depth of water have ye? Well now, sound; and ye'll just find so or so many fathoms,' as the case might be; and the obnoxious passenger was generally right. On one occasion, as the ship was going into Corfu, Sir Thomas came up the hatchway and cast his eyes towards the gallows. 'Bangham' - Charles Jenkin heard him say to his aide-de-camp, Lord Bangham - 'where the devil is that other chap? I left four fellows hanging there; now I can only see three. Mind there is another there to-morrow.' And sure enough there was another Greek dangling the next day. 'Captain Hamilton, of the CAMBRIAN, kept the Greeks in order afloat,' writes my author, 'and King Tom ashore.'

From 1823 onward, the chief scene of Charles Jenkin's activities was in the West Indies, where he was engaged off and on till 1844, now as a subaltern, now in a vessel of his own, hunting out pirates, 'then very notorious' in the Leeward Islands, cruising after slavers, or carrying dollars and provisions for the Government. While yet a midshipman, he accompanied Mr. Cockburn to Caraccas and had a sight of Bolivar. In the brigantine GRIFFON, which he commanded in his last years in the West Indies, he carried aid to Guadeloupe after the earthquake, and twice earned the thanks of Government: once for an expedition to Nicaragua to extort, under threat of a blockade, proper apologies and a sum of money due to certain British merchants; and once during an insurrection in San Domingo, for the rescue of certain others from a perilous imprisonment and the recovery of a 'chest of money' of which they had been robbed. Once, on the other hand, he earned his share of public censure. This was in 1837, when he commanded the ROMNEY lying in the inner harbour of Havannah. The ROMNEY was in no proper sense a man-of-war; she was a slave-hulk, the bonded warehouse of the Mixed Slave Commission; where negroes, captured out of slavers under Spanish colours, were detained provisionally, till the Commission should decide upon their case and either set them free or bind them to apprenticeship. To this ship. already an eye-sore to the authorities, a Cuban slave made his escape. The position was invidious; on one side were the tradition of the British flag and the state of public sentiment at home; on the other, the certainty that if the slave were kept, the ROMNEY would be ordered at once out of the harbour, and the object of the Mixed Commission compromised. Without consultation with any other officer, Captain Jenkin (then lieutenant) returned the man to shore and took the Captain-General's receipt. Lord Palmerston approved his course; but the zealots of the anti-slave trade movement (never to be named without respect) were much dissatisfied; and thirty-nine years later, the matter was again canvassed in Parliament, and Lord Palmerston and Captain Jenkin defended by Admiral Erskine in a letter to the TIMES (March 13, 1876).

In 1845, while still lieutenant, Charles Jenkin acted as Admiral Pigot's flag captain in the Cove of Cork, where there were some thirty pennants; and about the same time, closed his career by an act of personal bravery. He had proceeded with his boats to the help of a merchant vessel, whose cargo of combustibles had taken fire and was smouldering under hatches; his sailors were in the hold, where the fumes were already heavy, and Jenkin was on deck directing operations, when he found his orders were no longer answered from below: he jumped down without hesitation and slung up several insensible men with his own hand. For this act, he received a letter from the Lords of the Admiralty expressing a sense of his gallantry; and pretty soon after was promoted Commander, superseded, and could never again obtain employment.
In 1828 or 1829, Charles Jenkin was in the same watch with another midshipman, Robert Colin Campbell Jackson, who introduced him to his family in Jamaica. The father, the Honourable Robert Jackson, Custos Rotulorum of Kingston, came of a Yorkshire family, said to be originally Scotch; and on the mother's side, counted kinship with some of the Forbeses. The mother was Susan Campbell, one of the Campbells of Auchenbreck. Her father Colin, a merchant in Greenock, is said to have been the heir to both the estate and the baronetcy; he claimed neither, which

casts a doubt upon the fact, but he had pride enough himself, and taught enough pride to his family, for any station or descent in Christendom. He had four daughters. One married an Edinburgh writer, as I have it on a first account - a minister, according to another - a man at least of reasonable station, but not good enough for the Campbells of Auchenbreck; and the erring one was instantly discarded. Another married an actor of the name of Adcock, whom (as I receive the tale) she had seen acting in a barn; but the phrase should perhaps be regarded rather as a measure of the family annoyance, than a mirror of the facts. The marriage was not in itself unhappy; Adcock was a gentleman by birth and made a good husband; the family reasonably prospered, and one of the daughters married no less a man than Clarkson Stanfield. But by the father, and the two remaining Miss Campbells, people of fierce passions and a truly Highland pride, the derogation was bitterly resented. For long the sisters lived estranged then, Mrs. Jackson and Mrs. Adcock were reconciled for a moment, only to quarrel the more fiercely; the name of Mrs. Adcock was proscribed, nor did it again pass her sister's lips, until the morning when she announced: 'Mary Adcock is dead; I saw her in her shroud last night.' Second sight was hereditary in the house; and sure enough, as I have it reported, on that very night Mrs. Adcock had passed away. Thus, of the four daughters, two had, according to the idiotic notions of their friends, disgraced themselves in marriage; the others supported the honour of the family with a better grace, and married West Indian magnates of whom, I believe, the world has never heard and would not care to hear: So strange a thing is this hereditary pride. Of Mr. Jackson, beyond the fact that he was Fleeming's grandfather, I know naught. His wife, as I have said, was a woman of fierce passions; she would tie her house slaves to the bed and lash them with her own hand; and her conduct to her wild and down-going sons, was a mixture of almost insane self-sacrifice and wholly insane violence of temper. She had three sons and one daughter. Two of the sons went utterly to ruin, and reduced their mother to poverty. The third went to India, a slim, delicate lad, and passed so wholly from the knowledge of his relatives that he was thought to be long dead. Years later, when his sister was living in Genoa, a red-bearded man of great strength and stature, tanned by years in India, and his hands covered with barbaric gems, entered the room unannounced, as she was playing the piano, lifted her from her seat, and kissed her. It was her brother, suddenly returned out of a past that was never very clearly understood, with the rank of general, many strange gems, many cloudy stories of adventure, and next his heart, the daguerreotype of an Indian prince with whom he had mixed blood.

The last of this wild family, the daughter, Henrietta Camilla, became the wife of the midshipman Charles, and the mother of the subject of this notice, Fleeming Jenkin. She was a woman of parts and courage. Not beautiful, she had a far higher gift, the art of seeming so; played the part of a belle in society, while far lovelier women were left unattended; and up to old age had much of both the exigency and the charm that mark that character. She drew naturally, for she had no training, with unusual skill; and it was from her, and not from the two naval artists, that Fleeming inherited his eye and hand. She played on the harp and sang with something beyond the talent of an amateur. At the age of seventeen, she heard Pasta in Paris; flew up in a fire of youthful enthusiasm; and the next morning, all alone and without introduction, found her way into the presence of the PRIMA DONNA and begged for lessons. Pasta made her sing, kissed her when she had done, and though she refused to be her mistress, placed her in the hands of a friend. Nor was this all, for when Pasta returned to Paris, she sent for the girl (once at least) to test her progress. But Mrs. Jenkin's talents were not so remarkable as her fortitude and strength of will; and it was in an art for which she had no natural taste (the art of literature) that she appeared before the public. Her novels, though they attained and merited a certain popularity both in France and England, are a measure only of her courage. They were a task, not a beloved task; they were written for money in days of poverty, and they served their end. In the least thing as well as in the greatest, in every province of life as well as in her novels, she displayed the same capacity of taking infinite pains, which descended to her son. When she was about forty (as near as her age was known) she lost her voice; set herself at once to learn the piano, working eight hours a day; and attained to such proficiency that her collaboration in chamber music was courted by professionals. And more than twenty years later, the old lady might have been seen dauntlessly beginning the study of Hebrew. This is the more ethereal part of courage; nor was she wanting in the more material. Once when a neighbouring groom, a married man, had seduced her maid, Mrs. Jenkin mounted her horse, rode over to the stable entrance and horsewhipped the man with her own hand.

How a match came about between this talented and spirited girl and the young midshipman, is not very I easy to conceive. Charles Jenkin was one of the finest creatures breathing; loyalty, devotion, simple natural piety, boyish cheerfulness, tender and manly sentiment in the old sailor fashion, were in him inherent and inextinguishable either by age, suffering, or injustice. He looked, as he was, every inch a gentleman; he must have been everywhere notable, even among handsome men, both for his face and his gallant bearing; not so much that of a sailor, you would have said, as like one of those gentle and graceful soldiers that, to this day, are the most pleasant of Englishmen to see. But though he was in these ways noble, the dunce scholar of Northiam was to the end no genius. Upon all points that a man must understand to be a gentleman, to be upright, gallant, affectionate and dead to self, Captain Jenkin was more knowing than one among a thousand; outside of that, his mind was very largely blank. He had indeed a simplicity that came near to vacancy; and in the first forty years of his married life, this want grew more accentuated. In both families imprudent marriages had been the rule; but neither Jenkin nor Campbell had ever entered into a more unequal union. It was the captain's good looks, we may suppose, that gained for him this elevation; and in some ways and for many years of his life, he had to pay the penalty. His wife, impatient of his incapacity and surrounded by brilliant friends, used him with a certain contempt. She was the managing partner; the life was hers, not his; after his retirement they lived much abroad, where the poor captain, who could never learn any language but his own, sat in the corner mumchance; and even his son, carried away by his bright mother, did not recognise for long the treasures of simple chivalry that lay buried in the heart of his father. Yet it would be an error to regard this marriage as unfortunate. It not only lasted long enough to justify itself in a beautiful and touching epilogue, but it gave to the world the scientific work and what (while time was) were of far greater value, the delightful qualities of Fleeming Jenkin. The Kentish-Welsh family, facile, extravagant, generous to a fault and far from brilliant, had given the father, an extreme example of its humble virtues. On the other side, the wild, cruel, proud, and somewhat blackguard stock of the Scotch Campbell-Jacksons, had put forth, in the person of the mother all its force and courage.

The marriage fell in evil days. In 1823, the bubble of the Golden Aunt's inheritance had burst. She died holding the hand of the nephew she had so wantonly deceived; at the last she drew him down and seemed to bless him, surely with some remorseful feeling; for when the will was opened, there was not found so much as the mention of his name. He was deeply in debt; in debt even to the estate of his deceiver, so that he had to sell a piece of land to clear himself. 'My dear boy,' he said to Charles, 'there will be nothing left for you. I am a ruined man.' And here follows for me the strangest part of this story. From the death of the treacherous aunt, Charles Jenkin, senior, had still some nine years to live; it was perhaps too late for him to turn to saving, and perhaps his affairs were past restoration. But his family at least had all this while to prepare; they were still young men, and knew what they had to look for at their father's death; and yet when that happened in September, 1831, the heir was still apathetically waiting. Poor John, the days of his whips and spurs, and Yeomanry dinners, were quite over; and with that incredible softness of the Jenkin nature, he settled down for the rest of a long life, into something not far removed above a peasant. The mill farm at Stowting had been saved out of the wreck; and here he built himself a house on the Mexican model, and made the two ends meet with rustic thrift, gathering dung with his own hands upon the road and not at all abashed at his employment. In dress, voice, and manner, he fell into mere country plainness; lived without the least care for appearances, the least regret for the past or discontentment with the present; and when he came to die, died with Stoic cheerfulness, announcing that he had had a comfortable time and was yet well pleased to go. One would think there was little active virtue to be inherited from such a race; and yet in this same voluntary peasant, the special gift of Fleeming Jenkin was already half developed. The old man to the end was perpetually inventing; his strange, ill-spelled, unpunctuated correspondence is full (when he does not drop into cookery receipts) of pumps, road engines, steam-diggers, steam-ploughs, and steam-threshing machines; and I have it on Fleeming's word that what he did was full of ingenuity - only, as if by some cross destiny, useless. These disappointments he not only took with imperturbable good humour, but rejoiced with a particular relish over his nephew's success in the same field. 'I glory in the professor,' he wrote to his brother; and to Fleeming himself, with a touch of simple drollery, 'I was much pleased with your lecture, but why did you hit me so hard with Conisure's' (connoisseur's, QUASI amateur's) 'engineering? Oh, what presumption! - either of you or MYself!' A quaint, pathetic figure, this of uncle John, with his dung cart and his inventions; and the romantic fancy of his Mexican house; and his craze about the Lost Tribes which seemed to the worthy man the key of all perplexities; and his quiet conscience, looking back on a life not altogether vain, for he was a good son to his father while his father lived, and when evil days approached, he had proved himself a cheerful Stoic.

It followed from John's inertia, that the duty of winding up the estate fell into the hands of Charles. He managed it with no more skill than might be expected of a sailor ashore, saved a bare livelihood for John and nothing for the rest. Eight months later, he married Miss Jackson; and with her money, bought in some two-thirds of Stowting. In the beginning of the little family history which I have been following to so great an extent, the Captain mentions, with a delightful pride: 'A Court Baron and Court Leet are regularly held by the Lady of the Manor, Mrs. Henrietta Camilla Jenkin'; and indeed the pleasure of so describing his wife, was the most solid benefit of the investment; for the purchase was heavily encumbered and paid them nothing till some years before their death. In the meanwhile, the Jackson family also, what with wild sons, an indulgent mother and the impending emancipation of the slaves, was moving nearer and nearer to beggary; and thus of two doomed and declining houses, the subject of this memoir was born, heir to an estate and to no money, yet with inherited qualities that were to make him known and loved.

CHAPTER II. 1833-1851.

Birth and Childhood - Edinburgh - Frankfort-on-the-Main - Paris - The Revolution of 1848 - The Insurrection - Flight to Italy - Sympathy with Italy - The Insurrection in Genoa - A Student in Genoa - The Lad and his Mother.

HENRY CHARLES FLEEMING JENKIN (Fleeming, pronounced Flemming, to his friends and family) was born in a Government building on the coast of Kent, near Dungeness, where his father was serving at the time in the Coastguard, on March 25, 1833, and named after Admiral Fleeming, one of his father's protectors in the navy.

His childhood was vagrant like his life. Once he was left in the care of his grandmother Jackson, while Mrs. Jenkin sailed in her husband's ship and stayed a year at the Havannah. The tragic woman was besides from time to time a member of the family she was in distress of mind and reduced in fortune by the misconduct of her sons; her destitution and solitude made it a recurring duty to receive her, her violence continually enforced fresh separations. In her passion of a disappointed mother, she was a fit object of pity; but her grandson, who heard her load his own mother with cruel insults and reproaches, conceived for her an indignant and impatient hatred, for which he blamed himself in later life. It is strange from this point of view to see his childish letters to Mrs. Jackson; and to think that a man, distinguished above all by stubborn truthfulness, should have been brought up to such dissimulation. But this is of course unavoidable in life; it did no harm to Jenkin; and whether he got harm or benefit from a so early acquaintance with violent and hateful scenes, is more than I can guess. The experience, at least, was formative; and in judging his character it should not be forgotten. But Mrs. Jackson was not the only stranger in their gates; the Captain's sister, Aunt Anna Jenkin, lived with them until her death; she had all the Jenkin beauty of countenance, though she was unhappily deformed in body and of frail health; and she even excelled her gentle and ineffectual family in all amiable qualities. So that each of the two races from which Fleeming sprang, had an outpost by his very cradle; the one he instinctively loved, the other hated; and the life-long war in his members had begun thus early by a victory for what was best.

We can trace the family from one country place to another in the south of Scotland; where the child learned his taste for sport by riding home the pony from the moors. Before he was nine he could write such a passage as this about a Hallowe'en observance: 'I pulled a middling-sized cabbage-runt with a pretty sum of gold about it. No witches would run after me when I was sowing my hempseed this year; my nuts blazed away together very comfortably to the end of their lives, and when mamma put hers in which were meant for herself and papa they blazed away in the like manner.' Before he was ten he could write, with a really irritating precocity, that he had been 'making some pictures from a book called "Les Francais peints par euxmemes." . . . It is full of pictures of all classes, with a description of each in French. The pictures are a little caricatured, but not much.' Doubtless this was only an echo from his mother, but it shows the atmosphere in which he breathed. It must have been a good change for this art critic to be the playmate of Mary Macdonald, their gardener's daughter at Barjarg, and to sup with her family on potatoes and milk; and Fleeming himself attached some value to this early and friendly experience of another class.

His education, in the formal sense, began at Jedburgh. Thence he went to the Edinburgh Academy, where he was the classmate of Tait and Clerk Maxwell, bore away many prizes, and was once unjustly flogged by Rector Williams. He used to insist that all his bad schoolfellows had died early, a belief amusingly characteristic of the man's consistent optimism. In 1846 the mother and son proceeded to Frankfort-on-the-Main, where they were soon joined by the father, now reduced to inaction and to play something like third fiddle in his narrow household. The emancipation of the slaves had deprived them of their last resource beyond the half-pay of a captain; and life abroad was not only desirable for the sake of Fleeming's education, it was almost enforced by reasons of economy. But it was, no doubt, somewhat hard upon the captain. Certainly that perennial boy found a companion in his son; they were both active and eager, both willing to be amused, both young, if not in years, then in character. They went out together on excursions and sketched old castles, sitting side by side; they had an angry rivalry in walking, doubtless equally sincere upon both sides; and indeed we may say that Fleeming was exceptionally favoured, and that no boy had ever a companion more innocent, engaging, gay, and airy. But although in this case it would be easy to exaggerate its import, yet, in the Jenkin family also, the tragedy of the generations was proceeding, and the child was growing out of his father's knowledge. His artistic aptitude was of a different order. Already he had his quick sight of many sides of life; he already overflowed with distinctions and generalisations, contrasting the dramatic art and national character of England, Germany, Italy, and France. If he were dull, he would write stories and poems. 'I have written,' he says at thirteen, 'a very long story in heroic measure, 300 lines, and another Scotch story and innumerable bits of poetry'; and at the same age he had not only a keen feeling for scenery, but could do something with his pen to call it up. I feel I do always less than justice to the delightful memory of Captain Jenkin; but with a lad of this character, cutting the teeth of his intelligence, he was sure to fall into the background.

The family removed in 1847 to Paris, where Fleeming was put to school under one Deluc. There he learned French, and (if the captain is right) first began to show a taste for mathematics. But a far more important teacher than Deluc was at hand; the year 1848, so momentous for Europe, was momentous also for Fleeming's character. The family politics were Liberal; Mrs. Jenkin, generous before all things, was sure to be upon the side of exiles; and in the house of a Paris friend of hers, Mrs. Turner - already known to fame as Shelley's Cornelia de Boinville - Fleeming saw and heard such men as Manin, Gioberti, and the Ruffinis. He was thus prepared to sympathise with revolution; and when the hour came, and he found himself in the midst of stirring and influential events, the lad's whole character was moved. He corresponded at that time with a young Edinburgh friend, one Frank Scott; and I am here going to draw somewhat largely on this boyish correspondence. It gives us at once a picture of the Revolution and a portrait of Jenkin at fifteen; not so different (his friends will think) from the Jenkin of the end - boyish, simple, opinionated, delighting in action, delighting before all things in any generous sentiment.

'February 23, 1848.

'When at 7 o'clock to-day I went out, I met a large band going round the streets, calling on the inhabitants to illuminate their houses, and bearing torches. This was all very good fun, and everybody was delighted; but as they stopped rather long and were rather turbulent in the Place de la Madeleine, near where we live' [in the Rue Caumartin] 'a squadron of dragoons came up, formed, and charged at a hand-gallop. This was a very pretty sight; the crowd was not too thick, so they easily got away; and the dragoons only gave blows with the back of the sword, which hurt but did not wound. I was as close to them as I am now to the other side of the table; it was rather impressive, however. At the second charge they rode on the pavement and knocked the torches out of the fellows' hands; rather a shame, too - wouldn't be stood in England. . . .

[At] 'ten minutes to ten . . . I went a long way along the Boulevards, passing by the office of Foreign Affairs, where Guizot lives, and where to-night there were about a thousand troops protecting him from the fury of the populace. After this was passed, the number of the people thickened, till about half a mile further on, I met a troop of vagabonds, the wildest vagabonds in the world - Paris vagabonds, well armed, having probably broken into gunsmiths' shops and taken the guns and swords. They were about a hundred. These were followed by about a thousand (I am rather diminishing than exaggerating numbers all through), indifferently armed with rusty sabres, sticks, etc. An uncountable troop of gentlemen, workmen, shopkeepers' wives (Paris women dare anything), ladies' maids, common women - in fact, a crowd of all classes, though by far the greater number were of the better dressed class - followed. Indeed, it was a splendid sight: the mob in front chanting the "MARSEILLAISE," the national war hymn, grave and powerful, sweetened by the night air - though night in these splendid streets was turned into day, every window was filled with lamps, dim torches were tossing in the crowd . . . for Guizot has late this night given in his resignation, and this was an improvised illumination.

'I and my father had turned with the crowd, and were close behind the second troop of vagabonds. Joy was on every face. I remarked to papa that "I would not have missed the scene for anything, I might never see such a splendid one," when PLONG went one shot - every face went pale - R-R-R-R-R went the whole detachment, [and] the whole crowd of gentlemen and ladies turned and cut. Such a scene! - ladies, gentlemen, and vagabonds went sprawling in the mud, not shot but tripped up; and those that went down could not rise, they were trampled over. . . . I ran a short time straight on and did not fall, then turned down a side street, ran fifty yards and felt tolerably safe; looked for papa, did not see him; so walked on quickly, giving the news as I went.' [It appears, from another letter, the boy was the first to carry word of the firing to the Rue St. Honore; and that his news wherever he brought it was received with hurrahs. It was an odd entrance upon life for a little English lad, thus to play the part of rumour in such a crisis of the history of France.]

'But now a new fear came over me. I had little doubt but my papa was safe, but my fear was that he should arrive at home before me and tell the story; in that case I knew my mamma would go half mad with fright, so on I went as quick as possible. I heard no more discharges. When I got half way home, I found my way blocked up by troops. That way or the Boulevards I must pass. In the Boulevards they were fighting, and I was afraid all other passages might be blocked up . . . and I should have to sleep in a hotel in that case, and then my mamma - however, after a long DETOUR, I found a passage and ran home, and in our street joined papa.

'. . . I'll tell you to-morrow the other facts gathered from newspapers and papa. . . . Tonight I have given you what I have seen with my own eyes an hour ago, and began trembling with excitement and fear. If I have been too long on this one subject, it is because it is yet before my eyes.

'Monday, 24.

'It was that fire raised the people. There was fighting all through the night in the Rue Notre Dame de Lorette, on the Boulevards where they had been shot at, and at the Porte St. Denis. At ten o'clock, they resigned the house of the Minister of Foreign Affairs (where the disastrous volley was fired) to the people, who immediately took possession of it. I went to school, but [was] hardly there when the row in that quarter commenced. Barricades began to be fixed. Everyone was very grave now; the EXTERNES went away, but no one came to fetch me, so I had to stay. No lessons could go on. A troop of armed men took possession of the barricades, so it was supposed I should have to sleep there. The revolters came and asked for arms, but Deluc (head-master) is a National Guard, and he said he had only his own and he wanted them; but he said he would not fire on them. Then they asked for wine, which he gave them. They took good care not to get drunk, knowing they would not be able to fight. They were very polite and behaved extremely well.

'About 12 o'clock a servant came for a boy who lived near me, [and] Deluc thought it best to send me with him. We heard a good deal of firing near, but did not come across any of the parties. As we approached the railway, the barricades were no longer formed of palings, planks, or stones; but they had got all the omnibuses as they passed, sent the horses and passengers about their business, and turned them over. A double row of overturned coaches made a capital barricade, with a few paving stones.

'When I got home I found to my astonishment that in our fighting quarter it was much quieter. Mamma had just been out seeing the troops in the Place de la Concorde, when suddenly the Municipal Guard, now fairly exasperated, prevented the National Guard from proceeding, and fired at them; the National Guard had come with their muskets not loaded, but at length returned the fire. Mamma saw the National Guard fire. The Municipal Guard were round the corner. She was delighted for she saw no person killed, though many of the Municipals were. . . . .

'I immediately went out with my papa (mamma had

just come back with him) and went to the Place de la Concorde. There was an enormous quantity of troops in the Place. Suddenly the gates of the gardens of the Tuileries opened: we rushed forward, out galloped an enormous number of cuirassiers, in the middle of which were a couple of low carriages, said first to contain the Count de Paris and the Duchess of Orleans, but afterwards they said it was the King and Queen; and then I heard he had abdicated. I returned and gave the news.

'Went out again up the Boulevards. The house of the Minister of Foreign Affairs was filled with people and "HOTEL DU PEUPLE" written on it; the Boulevards were barricaded with fine old trees that were cut down and stretched all across the road. We went through a great many little streets, all strongly barricaded, and sentinels of the people at the principal of them. The streets were very unquiet, filled with armed men and women, for the troops had followed the ex-King to Neuilly and left Paris in the power of the people. We met the captain of the Third Legion of the National Guard (who had principally protected the people), badly wounded by a Municipal Guard, stretched on a litter. He was in possession of his senses. He was surrounded by a troop of men crying "Our brave captain - we have him yet - he's not dead! VIVE LA REFORME!" This cry was responded to by all, and every one saluted him as he passed. I do not know if he was mortally wounded. That Third Legion has behaved splendidly.

'I then returned, and shortly afterwards went out again to the garden of the Tuileries. They were given up to the people and the palace was being sacked. The people were firing blank cartridges to testify their joy, and they had a cannon on the top of the palace. It was a sight to see a palace sacked and armed vagabonds firing out of the windows, and throwing shirts, papers, and dresses of all kinds out of the windows. They are not rogues, these French; they are not stealing, burning, or doing much harm. In the Tuileries they have dressed up some of the statues, broken some, and stolen nothing but queer dresses. I say, Frank, you must not hate the French; hate the Germans if you like. The French laugh at us a little, and call out GODDAM in the streets; but to-day, in civil war, when they might have put a bullet through our heads, I never was insulted once.

'At present we have a provisional Government, consisting of Odion [SIC] Barrot, Lamartine, Marast, and some others; among them a common workman, but very intelligent. This is a triumph of liberty - rather!

'Now then, Frank, what do you think of it? I in a revolution and out all day. Just think, what fun! So it was at first, till I was fired at yesterday; but to-day I was not frightened, but it turned me sick at heart, I don't know why. There has been no great bloodshed, [though] I certainly have seen men's blood several times. But there's something shocking to see a whole armed populace, though not furious, for not one single shop has been broken open, except the gunsmiths' shops, and most of the arms will probably be taken back again. For the French have no cupidity in their nature; they don't like to steal - it is not in their nature. I shall send this letter in a day or two, when I am sure the post will go again. I know I have been a long time writing, but I hope you will find the matter of this letter interesting, as coming from a person resident on the spot; though probably you don't take much interest in the French, but I can think, write, and speak on no other subject.

'Feb. 25.

'There is no more fighting, the people have conquered; but the barricades are still kept up, and the people are in arms, more than ever fearing some new act of treachery on the part of the ex-King. The fight where I was was the principal cause of the Revolution. I was in little danger from the shot, for there was an immense crowd in front of me, though quite within gunshot. [By another letter, a hundred yards from the troops.] I wished I had stopped there.

'The Paris streets are filled with the most extraordinary crowds of men, women and children, ladies and gentlemen. Every person joyful. The bands of armed men are perfectly polite. Mamma and aunt to-day walked through armed crowds alone, that were firing blank cartridges in all directions. Every person made way with the greatest politeness, and one common man with a blouse, coming by accident against her immediately stopped to beg her pardon in the politest manner. There are few drunken men. The Tuileries is still being run over by the people; they only broke two things, a bust of Louis Philippe and one of Marshal Bugeaud, who fired on the people. . . . .

'I have been out all day again to-day, and precious tired I am. The Republican party seem the strongest, and are going about with red ribbons in their button-holes. . . . .

'The title of "Mister" is abandoned; they say nothing but "Citizen," and the people are shaking hands amazingly. They have got to the top of the public monuments, and, mingling with bronze or stone statues, five or six make a sort of TABLEAU VIVANT, the top man holding up the red flag of the Republic; and right well they do it, and very picturesque they look. I think I shall put this letter in the post to-morrow as we got a letter to-night.

(On Envelope.)

'M. Lamartine has now by his eloquence conquered the whole armed crowd of citizens threatening to kill him if he did not immediately proclaim the Republic and red flag. He said he could not yield to the citizens of Paris alone, that the whole country must be consulted; that he chose the tricolour, for it had followed and accompanied the triumphs of France all over the world, and that the red flag had only been dipped in the blood of the citizens. For sixty hours he has been quieting the people: he is at the head of everything. Don't be prejudiced, Frank, by what you see in the papers. The French have acted nobly, splendidly; there has been no brutality, plundering, or stealing. . . . I did not like the French before; but in this respect they are the finest people in the world. I am so glad to have been here.'

And there one could wish to stop with this apotheosis of liberty and order read with the generous enthusiasm of a boy; but as the reader knows, it was but the first act of the piece. The letters, vivid as they are, written as they were by a hand trembling with fear and excitement, yet do injustice, in their boyishness of tone, to the profound effect produced. At the sound of these songs and shot of cannon, the boy's mind awoke. He dated his own appreciation of the art of acting from the day when he saw and heard Rachel recite the

'MARSEILLAISE' at the Francais, the tricolour in her arms. What is still more strange, he had been up to then invincibly indifferent to music, insomuch that he could not distinguish 'God save the Queen' from 'Bonnie Dundee'; and now, to the chanting of the mob, he amazed his family by learning and singing 'MOURIR POUR LA PATRIE.' But the letters, though they prepare the mind for no such revolution in the boy's tastes and feelings, are yet full of entertaining traits. Let the reader note Fleeming's eagerness to influence his friend Frank, an incipient Tory (no less) as further history displayed; his unconscious indifference to his father and devotion to his mother, betrayed in so many significant expressions and omissions; the sense of dignity of this diminutive 'person resident on the spot,' who was so happy as to escape insult; and the strange picture of the household - father, mother, son, and even poor Aunt Anna - all day in the streets in the thick of this rough business, and the boy packed off alone to school in a distant quarter on the very morrow of the massacre.

They had all the gift of enjoying life's texture as it comes; they were all born optimists. The name of liberty was honoured in that family, its spirit also, but within stringent limits; and some of the foreign friends of Mrs. Jenkin were, as I have said, men distinguished on the Liberal side. Like Wordsworth, they beheld

France standing on the top of golden hours
And human nature seeming born again.

At once, by temper and belief, they were formed to find their element in such a decent and whiggish convulsion, spectacular in its course, moderate in its purpose. For them,

Bliss was it in that dawn to be alive,
But to be young was very heaven.

And I cannot but smile when I think that (again like Wordsworth) they should have so specially disliked the consequence.

It came upon them by surprise. Liberal friends of the precise right shade of colour had assured them, in Mrs. Turner's drawing-room, that all was for the best; and they rose on January 23 without fear. About the middle of the day they heard the sound of musketry, and the next morning they were wakened by the cannonade. The French who had behaved so 'splendidly,' pausing, at the voice of Lamartine, just where judicious Liberals could have desired - the French, who had 'no cupidity in their nature,' were now about to play a variation on the theme rebellion. The Jenkins took refuge in the house of Mrs. Turner, the house of the false prophets, 'Anna going with Mrs. Turner, that she might be prevented speaking English, Fleeming, Miss H. and I (it is the mother who writes) walking together. As we reached the Rue de Clichy, the report of the cannon sounded close to our ears and made our hearts sick, I assure you. The fighting was at the barrier Rochechouart, a few streets off. All Saturday and Sunday we were a prey to great alarm, there came so many reports that the insurgents were getting the upper hand. One could tell the state of affairs from the extreme quiet or the sudden hum in the street. When the news was bad, all the houses closed and the people disappeared; when better, the doors half opened and you heard the sound of men again. From the upper windows we could see each discharge from the Bastille - I mean the smoke rising - and also the flames and smoke from the Boulevard la Chapelle. We were four ladies, and only

Fleeming by way of a man, and difficulty enough we had to keep him from joining the National Guards - his pride and spirit were both fired. You cannot picture to yourself the multitudes of soldiers, guards, and armed men of all sorts we watched - not close to the window, however, for such havoc had been made among them by the firing from the windows, that as the battalions marched by, they cried, "Fermez vos fenetres!" and it was very painful to watch their looks of anxiety and suspicion as they marched by.'

'The Revolution,' writes Fleeming to Frank Scott, 'was quite delightful: getting popped at and run at by horses, and giving sous for the wounded into little boxes guarded by the raggedest, picturesquest, delightfullest, sentinels; but the insurrection! ugh, I shudder to think at [SIC] it.' He found it 'not a bit of fun sitting boxed up in the house four days almost. . . I was the only GENTLEMAN to four ladies, and didn't they keep me in order! I did not dare to show my face at a window, for fear of catching a stray ball or being forced to enter the National Guard; [for] they would have it I was a man full-grown, French, and every way fit to fight. And my mamma was as bad as any of them; she that told me I was a coward last time if I stayed in the house a quarter of an hour! But I drew, examined the pistols, of which I found lots with caps, powder, and ball, while sometimes murderous intentions of killing a dozen insurgents and dying violently overpowered by numbers. . . . .' We may drop this sentence here: under the conduct of its boyish writer, it was to reach no legitimate end.

Four days of such a discipline had cured the family of Paris; the same year Fleeming was to write, in answer apparently to a question of Frank Scott's, 'I could find no national game in France but revolutions'; and the witticism was justified in their experience. On the first possible day, they applied for passports, and were advised to take the road to Geneva. It appears it was scarce safe to leave Paris for England. Charles Reade, with keen dramatic gusto, had just smuggled himself out of that city in the bottom of a cab. English gold had been found on the insurgents, the name of England was in evil odour; and it was thus - for strategic reasons, so to speak - that Fleming found himself on the way to that Italy where he was to complete his education, and for which he cherished to the end a special kindness.

It was in Genoa they settled; partly for the sake of the captain, who might there find naval comrades; partly because of the Ruffinis, who had been friends of Mrs. Jenkin in their time of exile and were now considerable men at home; partly, in fine, with hopes that Fleming might attend the University; in preparation for which he was put at once to school. It was the year of Novara; Mazzini was in Rome; the dry bones of Italy were moving; and for people of alert and liberal sympathies the time was inspiring. What with exiles turned Ministers of State, universities thrown open to Protestants, Fleming himself the first Protestant student in Genoa, and thus, as his mother writes, 'a living instance of the progress of liberal ideas' - it was little wonder if the enthusiastic young woman and the clever boy were heart and soul upon the side of Italy. It should not be forgotten that they were both on their first visit to that country; the mother still child enough 'to be delighted when she saw real monks'; and both mother and son thrilling with the first sight of snowy Alps, the blue Mediterranean, and the crowded port and the palaces of Genoa. Nor was their zeal without knowledge. Ruffini, deputy for Genoa and soon to be head of the University, was at their side; and by means of him the family appear to have had access to much Italian society. To the end, Fleeming professed his admiration of the Piedmontese and his unalterable confidence in the future of Italy under their conduct; for Victor Emanuel, Cavour, the first La Marmora and Garibaldi, he had varying degrees of sympathy and praise: perhaps highest for the King, whose good sense and temper filled him with respect - perhaps least for Garibaldi, whom he loved but yet mistrusted.

But this is to look forward: these were the days not of Victor Emanuel but of Charles Albert; and it was on Charles Albert that mother and son had now fixed their eyes as on the sword-bearer of Italy. On Fleeming's sixteenth birthday, they were, the mother writes, 'in great anxiety for news from the army. You can have no idea what it is to live in a country where such a struggle is going on. The interest is one that absorbs all others. We eat, drink, and sleep to the noise of drums and musketry. You would enjoy and almost admire Fleeming's enthusiasm and earnestness - and, courage, I may say - for we are among the small minority of English who side with the Italians. The other day, at dinner at the Consul's, boy as he is, and in spite of my admonitions, Fleeming defended the Italian cause, and so well that he "tripped up the heels of his adversary" simply from being well-informed on the subject and honest. He is as true as steel, and for no one will he bend right or left. . . . . Do not fancy him a Bobadil,' she adds, 'he is only a very true, candid boy. I am so glad he remains in all respects but information a great child.'

If this letter is correctly dated, the cause was already

lost and the King had already abdicated when these lines were written. No sooner did the news reach Genoa, than there began 'tumultuous movements'; and the Jenkins' received hints it would be wise to leave the city. But they had friends and interests; even the captain had English officers to keep him company, for Lord Hardwicke's ship, the VENGEANCE, lay in port; and supposing the danger to be real, I cannot but suspect the whole family of a divided purpose, prudence being possibly weaker than curiosity. Stay, at least, they did, and thus rounded their experience of the revolutionary year. On Sunday, April 1, Fleeming and the captain went for a ramble beyond the walls, leaving Aunt Anna and Mrs. Jenkin to walk on the bastions with some friends. On the way back, this party turned aside to rest in the Church of the Madonna delle Grazie. 'We had remarked,' writes Mrs. Jenkin, 'the entire absence of sentinels on the ramparts, and how the cannons were left in solitary state; and I had just remarked "How quiet everything is!" when suddenly we heard the drums begin to beat and distant shouts. ACCUSTOMED AS WE ARE to revolutions, we never thought of being frightened.' For all that, they resumed their return home. On the way they saw men running and vociferating, but nothing to indicate a general disturbance, until, near the Duke's palace, they came upon and passed a shouting mob dragging along with it three cannon. It had scarcely passed before they heard 'a rushing sound'; one of the gentlemen thrust back the party of ladies under a shed, and the mob passed again. A fine-looking young man was in their hands; and Mrs. Jenkin saw him with his mouth open as if he sought to speak, saw him tossed from one to another like a ball, and then saw him no more. 'He was dead a few instants after, but the crowd hid that terror from us. My knees shook under me and my sight left me.' With this street tragedy, the curtain rose upon their second revolution.

The attack on Spirito Santo, and the capitulation and departure of the troops speedily followed. Genoa was in the hands of the Republicans, and now came a time when the English residents were in a position to pay some return for hospitality received. Nor were they backward. Our Consul (the same who had the benefit of correction from Fleeming) carried the Intendente on board the VENGEANCE, escorting him through the streets, getting along with him on board a shore boat, and when the insurgents levelled their muskets, standing up and naming himself, 'CONSOLE INGLESE.' A friend of the Jenkins', Captain Glynne, had a more painful, if a less dramatic part. One Colonel Nosozzo had been killed (I read) while trying to prevent his own artillery from firing on the mob; but in that hell's cauldron of a distracted city, there were no distinctions made, and the Colonel's widow was hunted for her life. In her grief and peril, the Glynnes received and hid her; Captain Glynne sought and found her husband's body among the slain, saved it for two days, brought the widow a lock of the dead man's hair; but at last, the mob still strictly searching, seems to have abandoned the body, and conveyed his guest on board the VENGEANCE. The Jenkins also had their refugees, the family of an EMPLOYE threatened by a decree. 'You should have seen me making a Union Jack to nail over our door,' writes Mrs. Jenkin. 'I never worked so fast in my life. Monday and Tuesday,' she continues, 'were tolerably quiet, our hearts beating fast in the hope of La Marmora's approach, the streets barricaded, and none but foreigners and women allowed to leave the city.' On Wednesday, La Marmora came indeed, but in the ugly form of a bombardment;

and that evening the Jenkins sat without lights about their drawing-room window, 'watching the huge red flashes of the cannon' from the Brigato and La Specula forts, and hearkening, not without some awful pleasure, to the thunder of the cannonade.

Lord Hardwicke intervened between the rebels and La Marmora; and there followed a troubled armistice, filled with the voice of panic. Now the VENGEANCE was known to be cleared for action; now it was rumoured that the galley slaves were to be let loose upon the town, and now that the troops would enter it by storm. Crowds, trusting in the Union Jack over the Jenkins' door, came to beg them to receive their linen and other valuables; nor could their instances be refused; and in the midst of all this bustle and alarm, piles of goods must be examined and long inventories made. At last the captain decided things had gone too far. He himself apparently remained to watch over the linen; but at five o'clock on the Sunday morning, Aunt Anna, Fleeming, and his mother were rowed in a pour of rain on board an English merchantman, to suffer 'nine mortal hours of agonising suspense.' With the end of that time, peace was restored. On Tuesday morning officers with white flags appeared on the bastions; then, regiment by regiment, the troops marched in, two hundred men sleeping on the ground floor of the Jenkins' house, thirty thousand in all entering the city, but without disturbance, old La Marmora being a commander of a Roman sternness.

With the return of quiet, and the reopening of the universities, we behold a new character, Signor Flaminio: the professors, it appears, made no attempt upon the Jenkin; and thus readily italianised the Fleeming. He came well recommended; for their friend

Ruffini was then, or soon after, raised to be the head of the University; and the professors were very kind and attentive, possibly to Ruffini's PROTEGE, perhaps also to the first Protestant student. It was no joke for Signor Flaminio at first; certificates had to be got from Paris and from Rector Williams; the classics must be furbished up at home that he might follow Latin lectures; examinations bristled in the path, the entrance examination with Latin and English essay, and oral trials (much softened for the foreigner) in Horace, Tacitus, and Cicero, and the first University examination only three months later, in Italian eloquence, no less, and other wider subjects. On one point the first Protestant student was moved to thank his stars: that there was no Greek required for the degree. Little did he think, as he set down his gratitude, how much, in later life and among cribs and dictionaries, he was to lament this circumstance; nor how much of that later life he was to spend acquiring, with infinite toil, a shadow of what he might then have got with ease and fully. But if his Genoese education was in this particular imperfect, he was fortunate in the branches that more immediately touched on his career. The physical laboratory was the best mounted in Italy. Bancalari, the professor of natural philosophy, was famous in his day; by what seems even an odd coincidence, he went deeply into electromagnetism; and it was principally in that subject that Signor Flaminio, questioned in Latin and answering in Italian, passed his Master of Arts degree with first-class honours. That he had secured the notice of his teachers, one circumstance sufficiently proves. A philosophical society was started under the presidency of Mamiani, 'one of the examiners and one of the leaders of the Moderate party'; and out of five promising students brought forward by the professors to attend the sittings and present essays, Signor Flaminio was one. I cannot find that he ever read an essay; and indeed I think his hands were otherwise too full. He found his fellow-students 'not such a bad set of chaps,' and preferred the Piedmontese before the Genoese; but I suspect he mixed not very freely with either. Not only were his days filled with university work, but his spare hours were fully dedicated to the arts under the eye of a beloved task-mistress. He worked hard and well in the art school, where he obtained a silver medal 'for a couple of legs the size of life drawn from one of Raphael's cartoons.' His holidays were spent in sketching; his evenings, when they were free, at the theatre. Here at the opera he discovered besides a taste for a new art, the art of music; and it was, he wrote, 'as if he had found out a heaven on earth.' 'I am so anxious that whatever he professes to know, he should really perfectly possess,' his mother wrote, 'that I spare no pains'; neither to him nor to myself, she might have added. And so when he begged to be allowed to learn the piano, she started him with characteristic barbarity on the scales; and heard in consequence 'heart-rending groans' and saw 'anguished claspings of hands' as he lost his way among their arid intricacies.

In this picture of the lad at the piano, there is something, for the period, girlish. He was indeed his mother's boy; and it was fortunate his mother was not altogether feminine. She gave her son a womanly delicacy in morals, to a man's taste - to his own taste in later life - too finely spun, and perhaps more elegant than healthful. She encouraged him besides in drawing-room interests. But in other points her influence was manlike. Filled with the spirit of thoroughness, she taught him to make of the least of these accomplishments a virile task; and the teaching lasted him through life. Immersed as she was in the day's movements and buzzed about by leading Liberals, she handed on to him her creed in politics: an enduring kindness for Italy, and a loyalty, like that of many clever women, to the Liberal party with but small regard to men or measures. This attitude of mind used often to disappoint me in a man so fond of logic; but I see now how it was learned from the bright eyes of his mother and to the sound of the cannonades of 1848. To some of her defects, besides, she made him heir. Kind as was the bond that united her to her son, kind and even pretty, she was scarce a woman to adorn a home; loving as she did to shine; careless as she was of domestic, studious of public graces. She probably rejoiced to see the boy grow up in somewhat of the image of herself, generous, excessive, enthusiastic, external; catching at ideas, brandishing them when caught; fiery for the right, but always fiery; ready at fifteen to correct a consul, ready at fifty to explain to any artist his own art.

The defects and advantages of such a training were obvious in Fleeming throughout life. His thoroughness was not that of the patient scholar, but of an untrained woman with fits of passionate study; he had learned too much from dogma, given indeed by cherished lips; and precocious as he was in the use of the tools of the mind, he was truly backward in knowledge of life and of himself. Such as it was at least, his home and school training was now complete; and you are to conceive the lad as being formed in a household of meagre revenue, among foreign surroundings, and under the influence of an imperious drawing-room queen; from whom he learned a great refinement of morals, a strong sense of duty, much forwardness of bearing, all manner of studious and artistic interests, and many ready-made opinions which he embraced with a son's and a disciple's loyalty.

CHAPTER III. 1851-1858.

Return to England - Fleeming at Fairbairn's - Experience in a Strike - Dr. Bell and Greek Architecture - The Gaskells - Fleeming at Greenwich - The Austins - Fleeming and the Austins - His Engagement - Fleeming and Sir W. Thomson.

IN 1851, the year of Aunt Anna's death, the family left Genoa and came to Manchester, where Fleeming was entered in Fairbairn's works as an apprentice. From the palaces and Alps, the Mole, the blue Mediterranean, the humming lanes and the bright theatres of Genoa, he fell - and he was sharply conscious of the fall - to the dim skies and the foul ways of Manchester. England he found on his return 'a horrid place,' and there is no doubt the family found it a dear one. The story of the Jenkin finances is not easy to follow. The family, I am told, did not practice frugality, only lamented that it should be needful; and Mrs. Jenkin, who was always complaining of 'those dreadful bills,' was 'always a good deal dressed.' But at this time of the return to England, things must have gone further. A holiday tour of a fortnight, Fleeming feared would be beyond what he could afford, and he only projected it 'to have a castle in the air.' And there were actual pinches. Fresh from a warmer sun, he was obliged to go without a greatcoat, and learned on railway journeys to supply the place of one with wrappings of old newspaper.

From half-past eight till six, he must 'file and chip vigorously in a moleskin suit and infernally dirty.' The work was not new to him, for he had already passed some time in a Genoese shop; and to Fleeming no work was without interest. Whatever a man can do or know, he longed to know and do also. 'I never learned anything,' he wrote, 'not even standing on my head, but I found a use for it.' In the spare hours of his first telegraph voyage, to give an instance of his greed of knowledge, he meant 'to learn the whole art of navigation, every rope in the ship and how to handle her on any occasion'; and once when he was shown a young lady's holiday collection of seaweeds, he must cry out, 'It showed me my eyes had been idle.' Nor was his the case of the mere literary smatterer, content if he but learn the names of things. In him, to do and to do well, was even a dearer ambition than to know. Anything done well, any craft, despatch, or finish, delighted and inspired him. I remember him with a twopenny Japanese box of three drawers, so exactly fitted that, when one was driven home, the others started from their places; the whole spirit of Japan, he told me, was pictured in that box; that plain piece of carpentry was as much inspired by the spirit of perfection as the happiest drawing or the finest bronze; and he who could not enjoy it in the one was not fully able to enjoy it in the others. Thus, too, he found in Leonardo's engineering and anatomical drawings a perpetual feast; and of the former he spoke even with emotion. Nothing indeed annoyed Fleeming more than the attempt to separate the fine arts from the arts of handicraft; any definition or theory that failed to bring these two together, according to him, had missed the point; and the essence of the pleasure received lay in seeing things well done. Other qualities must be added; he was the last to deny that; but this, of perfect craft, was at the bottom of all. And on the other hand, a nail ill-driven, a joint ill-fitted, a tracing clumsily done, anything to which a man had set his hand and not set it aptly, moved him to shame and anger. With such a character, he would feel but little drudgery at Fairbairn's. There would be something daily to be done, slovenliness to be avoided, and a higher mark of skill to be attained; he would chip and file, as he had practiced scales, impatient of his own imperfection, but resolute to learn.

And there was another spring of delight. For he was now moving daily among those strange creations of man's brain, to some so abhorrent, to him of an interest so inexhaustible: in which iron, water, and fire are made to serve as slaves, now with a tread more powerful than an elephant's, and now with a touch more precise and dainty than a pianist's. The taste for machinery was one that I could never share with him, and he had a certain bitter pity for my weakness. Once when I had proved, for the hundredth time, the depth of this defect, he looked at me askance. 'And the best of the joke,' said he, 'is that he thinks himself quite a poet.' For to him the struggle of the engineer against brute forces and with inert allies, was nobly poetic. Habit never dulled in him the sense of the greatness of the aims and obstacles of his profession. Habit only sharpened his inventor's gusto in contrivance, in triumphant artifice, in the Odyssean subtleties, by which wires are taught to speak, and iron hands to weave, and the slender ship to brave and to outstrip the tempest. To the ignorant the great results alone are admirable; to the knowing, and to Fleeming in particular, rather the infinite device and sleight of hand that made them possible.

A notion was current at the time that, in such a shop as Fairbairn's, a pupil would never be popular unless he drank with the workmen and imitated them in speech and manner. Fleeming, who would do none of these things, they accepted as a friend and companion; and this was the subject of remark in Manchester, where some memory of it lingers till to-day. He thought it one of the advantages of his profession to be brought into a close relation with the working classes; and for the skilled artisan he had a great esteem, liking his company, his virtues, and his taste in some of the arts. But he knew the classes too well to regard them, like a platform speaker, in a lump. He drew, on the other hand, broad distinctions; and it was his profound sense of the difference between one working man and another that led him to devote so much time, in later days, to the furtherance of technical education. In 1852 he had occasion to see both men and masters at their worst, in the excitement of a strike; and very foolishly (after their custom) both would seem to have behaved. Beginning with a fair show of justice on either side, the masters stultified their cause by obstinate impolicy, and the men disgraced their order by acts of outrage. 'On Wednesday last,' writes Fleeming, 'about three thousand banded round Fairbairn's door at 6 o'clock: men, women, and children, factory boys and girls, the lowest of the low in a very low place. Orders came that no one was to leave the works; but the men inside (Knobsticks, as they are called) were precious hungry and thought they would venture. Two of my companions and myself went out with the very first, and had the full benefit of every possible groan and bad language.' But the police cleared a lane through the crowd, the pupils were suffered to escape unhurt, and only the Knobsticks followed home and kicked with clogs; so that Fleeming enjoyed, as we may say, for nothing, that fine thrill of expectant valour with which he had sallied forth into the mob. 'I never before felt myself so decidedly somebody, instead of nobody,' he wrote.

Outside as inside the works, he was 'pretty merry and well to do,' zealous in study, welcome to many friends, unwearied in loving-kindness to his mother. For some time he spent three nights a week with Dr. Bell, 'working away at certain geometrical methods of getting the Greek architectural proportions': a business after Fleeming's heart, for he was never so pleased as when he could marry his two devotions, art and science. This was besides, in all likelihood, the beginning of that love and intimate appreciation of things Greek, from the least to the greatest, from the AGAMEMMON (perhaps his favourite tragedy) down to the details of Grecian tailoring, which he used to express in his familiar phrase: 'The Greeks were the boys.' Dr. Bell - the son of George Joseph, the nephew of Sir Charles, and though he made less use of it than some, a sharer in the distinguished talents of his race - had hit upon the singular fact that certain geometrical intersections gave the proportions of the Doric order. Fleeming, under Dr. Bell's direction, applied the same method to the other orders, and again found the proportions accurately given. Numbers of diagrams were prepared; but the discovery was never given to the world, perhaps because of the dissensions that arose between the authors. For Dr. Bell believed that 'these intersections were in some way connected with, or symbolical of, the antagonistic forces at work'; but his pupil and helper, with characteristic trenchancy, brushed aside this mysticism, and interpreted the discovery as 'a geometrical method of dividing the spaces or (as might be said) of setting out the work, purely empirical and in no way connected with any laws of either force or beauty.' 'Many a hard and pleasant fight we had over it,' wrote Jenkin, in later years; 'and impertinent as it may seem, the pupil is still unconvinced by the arguments of the master.' I do not know about the antagonistic forces in the Doric order; in Fleeming they were plain enough; and the Bobadil of these affairs with Dr. Bell was still, like the corrector of Italian consuls, 'a great child in everything but information.' At the house of Colonel Cleather, he might be seen with a family of children; and with these, there was no word of the Greek orders; with these Fleeming was only an uproarious boy and an entertaining draughtsman; so that his coming was the signal for the young people to troop into the playroom, where sometimes the roof rang with romping, and sometimes they gathered quietly about him as he amused them with his pencil.

In another Manchester family, whose name will be familiar to my readers - that of the Gaskells, Fleeming was a frequent visitor. To Mrs. Gaskell, he would often bring his new ideas, a process that many of his later friends will understand and, in their own cases, remember. With the girls, he had 'constant fierce wrangles,' forcing them to reason out their thoughts and to explain their prepossessions; and I hear from Miss Gaskell that they used to wonder how he could throw all the ardour of his character into the smallest matters, and to admire his unselfish devotion to his parents. Of one of these wrangles, I have found a record most characteristic of the man. Fleeming had been laying down his doctrine that the end justifies the means, and that it is quite right 'to boast of your six men-servants to a burglar or to steal a knife to prevent a murder'; and the Miss Gaskells, with girlish loyalty to what is current, had rejected the heresy with indignation. From such passages-at-arms, many retire mortified and ruffled; but Fleeming had no sooner left the house than he fell into delighted admiration of the spirit of his adversaries. From that it was but a step to ask himself 'what truth was sticking in their heads'; for even the falsest form of words (in Fleeming's life-long opinion) reposed upon some truth, just as he could 'not even allow that people admire ugly things, they admire what is pretty in the ugly thing.' And before he sat down to write his letter, he thought he had hit upon the explanation. 'I fancy the true idea,' he wrote, 'is that you must never do yourself or anyone else a moral injury - make any man a thief or a liar - for any end'; quite a different thing, as he would have loved to point out, from never stealing or lying. But this perfervid disputant was not always out of key with his audience. One whom he met in the same house announced that she would never again be happy. 'What does that signify?' cried Fleeming. 'We are not here to be happy, but to be good.' And the words (as his hearer writes to me) became to her a sort of motto during life.

From Fairbairn's and Manchester, Fleeming passed to a railway survey in Switzerland, and thence again to Mr. Penn's at Greenwich, where he was engaged as draughtsman. There in 1856, we find him in 'a terribly busy state, finishing up engines for innumerable gunboats and steam frigates for the ensuing campaign.' From half-past eight in the morning till nine or ten at night, he worked in a crowded office among uncongenial comrades, 'saluted by chaff, generally low personal and not witty,' pelted with oranges and apples, regaled with dirty stories, and seeking to suit himself with his surroundings or (as he writes it) trying to be as little like himself as possible. His lodgings were hard by, 'across a dirty green and through some half-built streets of two-storied houses'; he had Carlyle and the poets, engineering and mathematics, to study by himself in such spare time as remained to him; and there were several ladies, young and not so young, with whom he liked to correspond. But not all of these could compensate for the absence of that mother, who had made herself so large figure in his life, for sorry surroundings, unsuitable society, and work that leaned to the mechanical. 'Sunday,' says he, 'I generally visit some friends in town and seem to swim in clearer water, but the dirty green seems all the dirtier when I get back. Luckily I am fond of my profession, or I could not stand this life.' It is a question in my mind, if he could have long continued to stand it without loss. 'We are not here to be happy, but to be good,' quoth the young philosopher; but no man had a keener appetite for happiness than Fleeming Jenkin. There is a time of life besides when apart from circumstances, few men are agreeable to their neighbours and still fewer to themselves; and it was at this stage that Fleeming had arrived, later than common and even worse provided. The letter from which I have quoted is the last of his correspondence with Frank Scott, and his last confidential letter to one of his own sex. 'If you consider it rightly,' he wrote long after, 'you will find the want of correspondence no such strange want in men's friendships. There is, believe me, something noble in the metal which does not rust though not burnished by daily use.' It is well said; but the last letter to Frank Scott is scarcely of a noble metal. It is plain the writer has outgrown his old self, yet not made acquaintance with the new. This letter from a busy youth of three and twenty, breathes of seventeen: the sickening alternations of conceit and shame, the expense of hope IN VACUO, the lack of friends, the longing after love; the whole world of egoism under which youth stands groaning, a voluntary Atlas.

With Fleeming this disease was never seemingly severe. The very day before this (to me) distasteful letter, he had written to Miss Bell of Manchester in a sweeter strain; I do not quote the one, I quote the other; fair things are the best. 'I keep my own little lodgings,' he writes, 'but come up every night to see mamma' (who was then on a visit to London) 'if not kept too late at the works; and have singing lessons once more, and sing "DONNE L'AMORE E SCALTRO PARGO-LETTO"; and think and talk about you; and listen to mamma's projects DE Stowting. Everything turns to gold at her touch, she's a fairy and no mistake. We go on talking till I have a picture in my head, and can hardly believe at the end that the original is Stowting. Even you don't know half how good mamma is; in other things too, which I must not mention. She teaches me how it is not necessary to be very rich to do much good. I begin to understand that mamma would find useful occupation and create beauty at the bottom of a volcano. She has little weaknesses, but is a real generous-hearted woman, which I suppose is the finest thing in the world.' Though neither mother nor son could be called beautiful, they make a pretty picture; the ugly, generous, ardent woman weaving rainbow illusions; the ugly, clear-sighted, loving son sitting at her side in one of his rare hours of pleasure, half-beguiled, half-amused, wholly admiring, as he listens. But as he goes home, and the fancy pictures fade, and Stowting is once more burthened with debt, and the noisy companions and the long hours of drudgery once more approach, no wonder if the dirty green seems all the dirtier or if Atlas must resume his load.

But in healthy natures, this time of moral teething passes quickly of itself, and is easily alleviated by fresh interests; and already, in the letter to Frank Scott, there are two words of hope: his friends in London, his love for his profession. The last might have saved him; for he was ere long to pass into a new sphere, where all his faculties were to be tried and exercised, and his life to be filled with interest and effort. But it was not left to engineering: another and more influential aim was to be set before him. He must, in any case, have fallen in love; in any case, his love would have ruled his life; and the question of choice was, for the descendant of two such families, a thing of paramount importance. Innocent of the world, fiery, generous, devoted as he was, the son of the wild Jacksons and the facile Jenkins might have been led far astray. By one of those partialities that fill men at once with gratitude and wonder, his choosing was directed well. Or are we to say that by a man's choice in marriage, as by a crucial merit, he deserves his fortune? One thing at least reason may discern: that a man but partly chooses, he also partly forms, his help-mate; and he must in part deserve her, or the treasure is but won for a moment to be lost. Fleeming chanced if you will (and indeed all these opportunities are as 'random as blind man's buff') upon a wife who was worthy of him; but he had the wit to know it, the courage to wait and labour for his prize, and the tenderness and chivalry that are required to keep such prizes precious. Upon this point he has himself written well, as usual with fervent optimism, but as usual (in his own phrase) with a truth sticking in his head.

'Love,' he wrote, 'is not an intuition of the person most suitable to us, most required by us; of the person with whom life flowers and bears fruit. If this were so, the chances of our meeting that person would be small indeed; our intuition would often fail; the blindness of love would then be fatal as it is proverbial. No, love works differently, and in its blindness lies its strength. Man and woman, each strongly desires to be loved, each opens to the other that heart of ideal aspirations which they have often hid till then; each, thus knowing the ideal of the other, tries to fulfil that ideal, each partially succeeds. The greater the love, the greater the success; the nobler the idea of each, the more durable, the more beautiful the effect. Meanwhile the blindness of each to the other's defects enables the transformation to proceed [unobserved,] so that when the veil is withdrawn (if it ever is, and this I do not know) neither knows that any change has occurred in the person whom they loved. Do not fear, therefore. I do not tell you that your friend will not change, but as I am sure that her choice cannot be that of a man with a base ideal, so I am sure the change will be a safe and a good one. Do not fear that anything you love will vanish, he must love it too.'

Among other introductions in London, Fleeming had presented a letter from Mrs. Gaskell to the Alfred Austins. This was a family certain to interest a thoughtful young man. Alfred, the youngest and least known of the Austins, had been a beautiful golden-haired child, petted and kept out of the way of both sport and study by a partial mother. Bred an attorney, he had (like both his brothers) changed his way of life, and was called to the bar when past thirty. A Commission of Enquiry into the state of the poor in Dorsetshire gave him an opportunity of proving his true talents; and he was appointed a Poor Law Inspector, first at Worcester, next at Manchester, where he had to deal with the potato famine and the

Irish immigration of the 'forties, and finally in London, where he again distinguished himself during an epidemic of cholera. He was then advanced to the Permanent Secretaryship of Her Majesty's Office of Works and Public Buildings; a position which he filled with perfect competence, but with an extreme of modesty; and on his retirement, in 1868, he was made a Companion of the Bath. While apprentice to a Norwich attorney, Alfred Austin was a frequent visitor in the house of Mr. Barron, a rallying place in those days of intellectual society. Edward Barron, the son of a rich saddler or leather merchant in the Borough, was a man typical of the time. When he was a child, he had once been patted on the head in his father's shop by no less a man than Samuel Johnson, as the Doctor went round the Borough canvassing for Mr. Thrale; and the child was true to this early consecration. 'A life of lettered ease spent in provincial retirement,' it is thus that the biographer of that remarkable man, William Taylor, announces his subject; and the phrase is equally descriptive of the life of Edward Barron. The pair were close friends, 'W. T. and a pipe render everything agreeable,' writes Barron in his diary in 1823; and in 1833, after Barron had moved to London and Taylor had tasted the first public failure of his powers, the latter wrote: 'To my ever dearest Mr. Barron say, if you please, that I miss him more than I regret him - that I acquiesce in his retirement from Norwich, because I could ill brook his observation of my increasing debility of mind.' This chosen companion of William Taylor must himself have been no ordinary man; and he was the friend besides of Borrow, whom I find him helping in his Latin. But he had no desire for popular distinction, lived privately, married a daughter of Dr. Enfield of Enfield's SPEAKER, and devoted his time to the education of his family, in a deliberate and scholarly fashion, and with certain traits of stoicism, that would surprise a modern. From these children we must single out his youngest daughter, Eliza, who learned under his care to be a sound Latin, an elegant Grecian, and to suppress emotion without outward sign after the manner of the Godwin school. This was the more notable, as the girl really derived from the Enfields; whose high-flown romantic temper, I wish I could find space to illustrate. She was but seven years old, when Alfred Austin remarked and fell in love with her; and the union thus early prepared was singularly full. Where the husband and wife differed, and they did so on momentous subjects, they differed with perfect temper and content; and in the conduct of life, and in depth and durability of love, they were at one. Each full of high spirits, each practised something of the same repression: no sharp word was uttered in their house. The same point of honour ruled them, a guest was sacred and stood within the pale from criticism. It was a house, besides, of unusual intellectual tension. Mrs. Austin remembered, in the early days of the marriage, the three brothers, John, Charles, and Alfred, marching to and fro, each with his hands behind his back, and 'reasoning high' till morning; and how, like Dr. Johnson, they would cheer their speculations with as many as fifteen cups of tea. And though, before the date of Fleeming's visit, the brothers were separated, Charles long ago retired from the world at Brandeston, and John already near his end in the 'rambling old house' at Weybridge, Alfred Austin and his wife were still a centre of much intellectual society, and still, as indeed they remained until the last, youthfully alert in mind. There was but one child of the marriage, Anne, and she was herself something new for the eyes of the young visitor; brought up, as she had been, like her mother before her, to the standard of a man's acquirements. Only one art had she been denied, she must not learn the violin - the thought was too monstrous even for the Austins; and indeed it would seem as if that tide of reform which we may date from the days of Mary Wollstonecraft had in some degree even receded; for though Miss Austin was suffered to learn Greek, the accomplishment was kept secret like a piece of guilt. But whether this stealth was caused by a backward movement in public thought since the time of Edward Barron, or by the change from enlightened Norwich to barbarian London, I have no means of judging.

When Fleeming presented his letter, he fell in love at first sight with Mrs. Austin and the life, and atmosphere of the house. There was in the society of the Austins, outward, stoical conformers to the world, something gravely suggestive of essential eccentricity, something unpretentiously breathing of intellectual effort, that could not fail to hit the fancy of this hot-brained boy. The unbroken enamel of courtesy, the self-restraint, the dignified kindness of these married folk, had besides a particular attraction for their visitor. He could not but compare what he saw, with what he knew of his mother and himself. Whatever virtues Fleeming possessed, he could never count on being civil; whatever brave, true-hearted qualities he was able to admire in Mrs. Jenkin, mildness of demeanour was not one of them. And here he found per sons who were the equals of his mother and himself in intellect and width of interest, and the equals of his father in mild urbanity of disposition. Show Fleeming an active virtue, and he always loved it. He went away from that house struck through with admiration, and vowing to himself that his own married life should be upon that pattern, his wife (whoever she might be) like Eliza Barron, himself such another husband as Alfred Austin. What is more strange, he not only brought away, but left behind him, golden opinions. He must have been - he was, I am told - a trying lad; but there shone out of him such a light of innocent candour, enthusiasm, intelligence, and appreciation, that to persons already some way forward in years, and thus able to enjoy indulgently the perennial comedy of youth, the sight of him was delightful. By a pleasant coincidence, there was one person in the house whom he did not appreciate and who did not appreciate him: Anne Austin, his future wife. His boyish vanity ruffled her; his appearance, never impressive, was then, by reason of obtrusive boyishness, still less so; she found occasion to put him in the wrong by correcting a false quantity; and when Mr. Austin, after doing his visitor the almost unheard-of honour of accompanying him to the door, announced 'That was what young men were like in my time' - she could only reply, looking on her handsome father, 'I thought they had been better looking.'

This first visit to the Austins took place in 1855; and it seems it was some time before Fleeming began to know his mind; and yet longer ere he ventured to show it. The corrected quantity, to those who knew him well, will seem to have played its part; he was the man always to reflect over a correction and to admire the castigator. And fall in love he did; not hurriedly but step by step, not blindly but with critical discrimination; not in the fashion of Romeo, but before he was done, with all Romeo's ardour and more than Romeo's faith. The high favour to which he presently rose in the esteem of Alfred Austin and his wife, might well give him ambitious notions; but the poverty of the present and the obscurity of the future were there to give him pause; and when his aspirations began to settle round Miss Austin, he tasted, perhaps for the only time in his life, the pangs of diffidence. There was indeed opening before him a wide door of hope. He had changed into the service of Messrs. Liddell & Gordon; these gentlemen had begun to dabble in the new field of marine telegraphy; and Fleeming was already face to face with his life's work. That impotent sense of his own value, as of a ship aground, which makes one of the agonies of youth, began to fall from him. New problems which he was endowed to solve, vistas of new enquiry which he was fitted to explore, opened before him continually. His gifts had found their avenue and goal. And with this pleasure of effective exercise, there must have sprung up at once the hope of what is called by the world success. But from these low beginnings, it was a far look upward to Miss Austin: the favour of the loved one seems always more than problematical to any lover; the consent of parents must be always more than doubtful to a young man with a small salary and no capital except capacity and hope. But Fleeming was not the lad to lose any good thing for the lack of trial; and at length, in the autumn of 1857, this boyish-sized, boyish-mannered, and superlatively ill-dressed young engineer, entered the house of the Austins, with such sinkings as we may fancy, and asked leave to pay his addresses to the daughter. Mrs. Austin already loved him like a son, she was but too glad to give him her consent; Mr. Austin reserved the right to inquire into his character; from neither was there a word about his prospects, by neither was his income mentioned. 'Are these people,' he wrote, struck with wonder at this dignified disinterestedness, 'are these people the same as other people?' It was not till he was armed with this permission, that Miss Austin even suspected the nature of his hopes: so strong, in this unmannerly boy, was the principle of true courtesy; so powerful, in this impetuous nature, the springs of self-repression. And yet a boy he was; a boy in heart and mind; and it was with a boy's chivalry and frankness that he won his wife. His conduct was a model of honour, hardly of tact; to conceal love from the loved one, to court her parents, to be silent and discreet till these are won, and then without preparation to approach the lady - these are not arts that I would recommend for imitation. They lead to final refusal. Nothing saved Fleeming from that fate, but one circumstance that cannot be counted upon - the hearty favour of the mother, and one gift that is inimitable and that never failed him throughout life, the gift of a nature essentially noble and outspoken. A happy and high-minded anger flashed through his despair: it won for him his wife.

Nearly two years passed before it was possible to marry: two years of activity, now in London; now at Birkenhead, fitting out ships, inventing new machinery for new purposes, and dipping into electrical experiment; now in the ELBA on his first telegraph cruise between Sardinia and Algiers: a busy and delightful period of bounding ardour, incessant toil, growing hope and fresh interests, with behind and through all, the image of his beloved. A few extracts from his correspondence with his betrothed will give the note of these truly joyous years. 'My profession gives me all the excitement and interest I ever hope for, but the sorry jade is obviously jealous of you.' - '"Poor Fleeming," in spite of wet, cold and wind, clambering over moist, tarry slips, wandering among pools of slush in waste places inhabited by wandering locomotives, grows visibly stronger, has dismissed his office cough and cured his toothache.' - 'The whole of the paying out and lifting machinery must be designed and ordered in two or three days, and I am half crazy with work. I like it though: it's like a good ball, the excitement carries you through.' - 'I was running to and from the ships and warehouse through fierce gusts of rain and wind till near eleven, and you cannot think what a pleasure it was to be blown about and think of you in your pretty dress.' - 'I am at the works till ten and sometimes till eleven. But I have a nice office to sit in, with a fire to myself, and bright brass scientific instruments all round me, and books to read, and experiments to make, and enjoy myself amazingly. I find the study of electricity so entertaining that I am apt to neglect my other work.' And for a last taste, 'Yesterday I had some charming electrical experiments. What shall I compare them to - a new song? a Greek play?'

It was at this time besides that he made the acquaintance of Professor, now Sir William, Thomson. To describe the part played by these two in each other's lives would lie out of my way. They worked together on the Committee on Electrical Standards; they served together at the laying down or the repair of many deep-sea cables; and Sir William was regarded by Fleeming, not only with the 'worship' (the word is his own) due to great scientific gifts, but with an ardour of personal friendship not frequently excelled. To their association, Fleeming brought the valuable element of a practical understanding; but he never thought or spoke of himself where Sir William was in question; and I recall quite in his last days, a singular instance of this modest loyalty to one whom he admired and loved. He drew up a paper, in a quite personal interest, of his own services; yet even here he must step out of his way, he must add, where it had no claim to be added, his opinion that, in their joint work, the contributions of Sir William had been always greatly the most valuable. Again, I shall not readily forget with what emotion he once told me an incident of their associated travels. On one of the mountain ledges of Madeira, Fleeming's pony bolted between Sir William. and the precipice above; by strange good fortune and thanks to the steadiness of Sir William's horse, no harm was done; but for the moment, Fleeming saw his friend hurled into the sea, and almost by his own act: it was a memory that haunted him.

CHAPTER IV. 1859-1868.

Fleeming's Marriage - His Married Life - Professional Difficulties - Life at Claygate - Illness of Mrs. F. Jenkin; and of Fleeming - Appointment to the Chair at Edinburgh.

ON Saturday, Feb. 26, 1859, profiting by a holiday of four days, Fleeming was married to Miss Austin at Northiam: a place connected not only with his own family but with that of his bride as well. By Tuesday morning, he was at work again, fitting out cableships at Birkenhead. Of the walk from his lodgings to the works, I find a graphic sketch in one of his letters: 'Out over the railway bridge, along a wide road raised to the level of a ground floor above the land, which, not being built upon, harbours puddles, ponds, pigs, and Irish hovels; - so to the dock warehouses, four huge piles of building with no windows, surrounded by a wall about twelve feet high - in through the large gates, round which hang twenty or thirty rusty Irish, playing pitch and toss and waiting for employment; - on along the railway, which came in at the same gates and which branches down between each vast block - past a pilot-engine butting refractory trucks into their places - on to the last block, [and] down the branch, sniffing the guano-scented air and detecting the old bones. The hartshorn flavour of the guano becomes very strong, as I near the docks where, across the ELBA'S decks, a huge vessel is discharging her cargo of the brown dust, and where huge vessels have been discharging that same cargo for the last five months.' This was the walk he took his young wife on the morrow of his return. She had been used to the society of lawyers and civil servants, moving in that circle which seems to itself the pivot of the nation and is in truth only a clique like another; and Fleeming was to her the nameless assistant of a nameless firm of engineers, doing his inglorious business, as she now saw for herself, among unsavoury surroundings. But when their walk brought them within view of the river, she beheld a sight to her of the most novel beauty: four great, sea-going ships dressed out with flags. 'How lovely!' she cried. 'What is it for?' - 'For you,' said Fleeming. Her surprise was only equalled by her pleasure. But perhaps, for what we may call private fame, there is no life like that of the engineer; who is a great man in out-of-the-way places, by the dockside or on the desert island or in populous ships, and remains quite unheard of in the coteries of London. And Fleeming had already made his mark among the few who had an opportunity of knowing him.

His marriage was the one decisive incident of his career; from that moment until the day of his death, he had one thought to which all the rest were tributary, the thought of his wife. No one could know him even slightly, and not remark the absorbing greatness of that sentiment; nor can any picture of the man be drawn that does not in proportion dwell upon it. This is a delicate task; but if we are to leave behind us (as we wish) some presentment of the friend we have lost, it is a task that must be undertaken.

For all his play of mind and fancy, for all his indulgence - and, as time went on, he grew indulgent

Fleeming had views of duty that were even stern. He was too shrewd a student of his fellow-men to remain long content with rigid formulae of conduct. Iron-bound, impersonal ethics, the procrustean bed of rules, he soon saw at their true value as the deification of averages. 'As to Miss (I declare I forget her name) being bad,' I find him writing, 'people only mean that she has broken the Decalogue - which is not at all the same thing. People who have kept in the high-road of Life really have less opportunity for taking a comprehensive view of it than those who have leaped over the hedges and strayed up the hills; not but what the hedges are very necessary, and our stray travellers often have a weary time of it. So, you may say, have those in the dusty roads.' Yet he was himself a very stern respecter of the hedgerows; sought safety and found dignity in the obvious path of conduct; and would palter with no simple and recognised duty of his epoch. Of marriage in particular, of the bond so formed, of the obligations incurred, of the debt men owe to their children, he conceived in a truly antique spirit: not to blame others, but to constrain himself. It was not to blame, I repeat, that he held these views; for others, he could make a large allowance; and yet he tacitly expected of his friends and his wife a high standard of behaviour. Nor was it always easy to wear the armour of that ideal.

Acting upon these beliefs; conceiving that he had indeed 'given himself' (in the full meaning of these words) for better, for worse; painfully alive to his defects of temper and deficiency in charm; resolute to make up for these; thinking last of himself: Fleeming was in some ways the very man to have made a noble, uphill fight of an unfortunate marriage. In other ways, it is true he was one of the most unfit for such a trial.

And it was his beautiful destiny to remain to the last hour the same absolute and romantic lover, who had shown to his new bride the flag-draped vessels in the Mersey. No fate is altogether easy; but trials are our touchstone, trials overcome our reward; and it was given to Fleeming to conquer. It was given to him to live for another, not as a task, but till the end as an enchanting pleasure. 'People may write novels,' he wrote in 1869, 'and other people may write poems, but not a man or woman among them can write to say how happy a man may be, who is desperately in love with his wife after ten years of marriage.' And again in 1885, after more than twenty-six years of marriage, and within but five weeks of his death: 'Your first letter from Bournemouth,' he wrote, 'gives me heavenly pleasure - for which I thank Heaven and you too - who are my heaven on earth.' The mind hesitates whether to say that such a man has been more good or more fortunate.

Any woman (it is the defect of her sex) comes sooner to the stable mind of maturity than any man; and Jenkin was to the end of a most deliberate growth. In the next chapter, when I come to deal with his telegraphic voyages and give some taste of his correspondence, the reader will still find him at twenty-five an arrant school-boy. His wife besides was more thoroughly educated than he. In many ways she was able to teach him, and he proud to be taught; in many ways she outshone him, and he delighted to be outshone. All these superiorities, and others that, after the manner of lovers, he no doubt forged for himself, added as time went on to the humility of his original love. Only once, in all I know of his career, did he show a touch of smallness. He could not learn to sing correctly; his wife told him so and desisted from her lessons; and the mortification was so sharply felt that for years he could not be induced to go to a concert, instanced himself as a typical man without an ear, and never sang again. I tell it; for the fact that this stood singular in his behaviour, and really amazed all who knew him, is the happiest way I can imagine to commend the tenor of his simplicity; and because it illustrates his feeling for his wife. Others were always welcome to laugh at him; if it amused them, or if it amused him, he would proceed undisturbed with his occupation, his vanity invulnerable. With his wife it was different: his wife had laughed at his singing; and for twenty years the fibre ached. Nothing, again, was more notable than the formal chivalry of this unmannered man to the person on earth with whom he was the most familiar. He was conscious of his own innate and often rasping vivacity and roughness and he was never forgetful of his first visit to the Austins and the vow he had registered on his return. There was thus an artificial element in his punctilio that at times might almost raise a smile. But it stood on noble grounds; for this was how he sought to shelter from his own petulance the woman who was to him the symbol of the household and to the end the beloved of his youth.

I wish in this chapter to chronicle small beer; taking a hasty glance at some ten years of married life and of professional struggle; and reserving till the next all the more interesting matter of his cruises. Of his achievements and their worth, it is not for me to speak: his friend and partner, Sir William Thomson, has contributed a note on the subject, which will be found in the Appendix, and to which I must refer the reader. He is to conceive in the meanwhile for himself Fleeming's manifold engagements: his service on the Committee on Electrical Standards, his lectures on electricity at Chatham, his chair at the London University, his partnership with Sir William Thomson and Mr. Varley in many ingenious patents, his growing credit with engineers and men of science; and he is to bear in mind that of all this activity and acquist of reputation, the immediate profit was scanty. Soon after his marriage, Fleeming had left the service of Messrs. Liddell & Gordon, and entered into a general engineering partnership with Mr. Forde, a gentleman in a good way of business. It was a fortunate partnership in this, that the parties retained their mutual respect unlessened and separated with regret; but men's affairs, like men, have their times of sickness, and by one of these unaccountable variations, for hard upon ten years the business was disappointing and the profits meagre. 'Inditing drafts of German railways which will never get made': it is thus I find Fleeming, not without a touch of bitterness, describe his occupation. Even the patents hung fire at first. There was no salary to rely on; children were coming and growing up; the prospect was often anxious. In the days of his courtship, Fleeming had written to Miss Austin a dissuasive picture of the trials of poverty, assuring her these were no figments but truly bitter to support; he told her this, he wrote, beforehand, so that when the pinch came and she suffered, she should not be disappointed in herself nor tempted to doubt her own magnanimity: a letter of admirable wisdom and solicitude. But now that the trouble came, he bore it very lightly. It was his principle, as he once prettily expressed it, 'to enjoy each day's happiness, as it arises, like birds or children.' His optimism, if driven out at the door, would come in again by the window; if it found nothing but blackness in the present, would hit upon some ground of consolation in the future or the past. And his courage and energy were indefatigable. In the year 1863, soon after the birth of their first son, they moved into a cottage at Claygate near Esher; and about this time, under manifold troubles both of money and health, I find him writing from abroad: 'The country will give us, please God, health and strength. I will love and cherish you more than ever, you shall go where you wish, you shall receive whom you wish - and as for money you shall have that too. I cannot be mistaken. I have now measured myself with many men. I do not feel weak, I do not feel that I shall fail. In many things I have succeeded, and I will in this. And meanwhile the time of waiting, which, please Heaven, shall not be long, shall also not be so bitter. Well, well, I promise much, and do not know at this moment how you and the dear child are. If he is but better, courage, my girl, for I see light.'

This cottage at Claygate stood just without the village, well surrounded with trees and commanding a pleasant view. A piece of the garden was turfed over to form a croquet green, and Fleeming became (I need scarce say) a very ardent player. He grew ardent, too, in gardening. This he took up at first to please his wife, having no natural inclination; but he had no sooner set his hand to it, than, like everything else he touched, it became with him a passion. He budded roses, he potted cuttings in the coach-house; if there came a change of weather at night, he would rise out of bed to protect his favourites; when he was thrown with a dull companion, it was enough for him to discover in the man a fellow gardener; on his travels, he would go out of his way to visit nurseries and gather hints; and to the end of his life, after other occupations prevented him putting his own hand to the spade, he drew up a yearly programme for his gardener, in which all details were regulated. He had begun by this time to write. His paper on Darwin, which had the merit of convincing on one point the philosopher himself, had indeed been written before this in London lodgings; but his pen was not idle at Claygate; and it was here he wrote (among other things) that review of 'FECUNDITY, FERTILITY, STERILITY, AND ALLIED TOPICS,' which Dr. Matthews Duncan prefixed by way of introduction to the second edition of the work. The mere act of writing seems to cheer the vanity of the most incompetent; but a correction accepted by Darwin, and a whole review borrowed and reprinted by Matthews Duncan are compliments of a rare strain, and to a man still unsuccessful must have been precious indeed. There was yet a third of the same kind in store for him; and when Munro himself owned that he had found instruction in the paper on Lucretius, we may say that Fleeming had been crowned in the capitol of reviewing.

Croquet, charades, Christmas magic lanterns for the village children, an amateur concert or a review article in the evening; plenty of hard work by day; regular visits to meetings of the British Association, from one of which I find him characteristically writing: 'I cannot say that I have had any amusement yet, but I am enjoying the dulness and dry bustle of the whole thing'; occasional visits abroad on business, when he would find the time to glean (as I have said) gardening hints for himself, and old folk-songs or new fashions of dress for his wife; and the continual study and care of his children: these were the chief elements of his life. Nor were friends wanting. Captain and Mrs. Jenkin, Mr. and Mrs. Austin, Clerk Maxwell, Miss Bell of Manchester, and others came to them on visits. Mr. Hertslet of the Foreign Office, his wife and his daughter, were neighbours and proved kind friends; in

1867 the Howitts came to Claygate and sought the society of 'the two bright, clever young people'; and in a house close by, Mr. Frederick Ricketts came to live with his family. Mr. Ricketts was a valued friend during his short life; and when he was lost with every circumstance of heroism in the LA PLATA, Fleeming mourned him sincerely.

I think I shall give the best idea of Fleeming in this time of his early married life, by a few sustained extracts from his letters to his wife, while she was absent on a visit in 1864.

'NOV. 11. - Sunday was too wet to walk to Isleworth, for which I was sorry, so I staid and went to Church and thought of you at Ardwick all through the Commandments, and heard Dr. - expound in a remarkable way a prophecy of St. Paul's about Roman Catholics, which MUTATIS MUTANDIS would do very well for Protestants in some parts. Then I made a little nursery of Borecole and Enfield market cabbage, grubbing in wet earth with leggings and gray coat on. Then I tidied up the coach-house to my own and Christine's admiration. Then encouraged by BOUTS-RIMES I wrote you a copy of verses; high time I think; I shall just save my tenth year of knowing my lady-love without inditing poetry or rhymes to her.

'Then I rummaged over the box with my father's letters and found interesting notes from myself. One I should say my first letter, which little Austin I should say would rejoice to see and shall see - with a drawing of a cottage and a spirited "cob." What was more to the purpose, I found with it a paste-cutter which Mary begged humbly for Christine and I generously gave this morning.

'Then I read some of Congreve. There are admirable scenes in the manner of Sheridan; all wit and no character, or rather one character in a great variety of situations and scenes. I could show you some scenes, but others are too coarse even for my stomach hardened by a course of French novels.

'All things look so happy for the rain.

'NOV. 16. - Verbenas looking well. . . . I am but a poor creature without you; I have naturally no spirit or fun or enterprise in me. Only a kind of mechanical capacity for ascertaining whether two really is half four, etc.; but when you are near me I can fancy that I too shine, and vainly suppose it to be my proper light; whereas by my extreme darkness when you are not by, it clearly can only be by a reflected brilliance that I seem aught but dull. Then for the moral part of me: if it were not for you and little Odden, I should feel by no means sure that I had any affection power in me. . . . Even the muscular me suffers a sad deterioration in your absence. I don't get up when I ought to, I have snoozed in my chair after dinner; I do not go in at the garden with my wonted vigour, and feel ten times as tired as usual with a walk in your absence; so you see, when you are not by, I am a person without ability, affections or vigour, but droop dull, selfish, and spiritless; can you wonder that I love you?

'NOV. 17. - . . . I am very glad we married young. I would not have missed these five years, no, not for any hopes; they are my own.

'NOV. 30. - I got through my Chatham lecture very fairly though almost all my apparatus went astray. I dined at the mess, and got home to Isleworth the same evening; your father very kindly sitting up for me.

'DEC. 1. - Back at dear Claygate. Many cuttings flourish, especially those which do honour to your hand. Your Californian annuals are up and about. Badger is fat, the grass green. . . .

'DEC. 3. - Odden will not talk of you, while you are away, having inherited, as I suspect, his father's way of declining to consider a subject which is painful, as your absence is. . . . I certainly should like to learn Greek and I think it would be a capital pastime for the long winter evenings. . . . How things are misrated! I declare croquet is a noble occupation compared to the pursuits of business men. As for so-called idleness - that is, one form of it - I vow it is the noblest aim of man. When idle, one can love, one can be good, feel kindly to all, devote oneself to others, be thankful for existence, educate one's mind, one's heart, one's body. When busy, as I am busy now or have been busy to-day, one feels just as you sometimes felt when you were too busy, owing to want of servants.

'DEC. 5. - On Sunday I was at Isleworth, chiefly engaged in playing with Odden. We had the most enchanting walk together through the brickfields. It was very muddy, and, as he remarked, not fit for Nanna, but fit for us MEN. The dreary waste of bared earth, thatched sheds and standing water, was a paradise to him; and when we walked up planks to deserted mixing and crushing mills, and actually saw where the clay was stirred with long iron prongs, and chalk or lime ground with "a tind of a mill," his expression of contentment and triumphant heroism knew no limit to its beauty. Of course on returning I found Mrs. Austin looking out at the door in an anxious manner, and thinking we had been out quite long enough. . . . I am reading Don Quixote chiefly and am his fervent admirer, but I am so sorry he did not place his affections on a Dulcinea of somewhat worthier stamp. In fact I think there must be a mistake about it. Don Quixote might and would serve his lady in most preposterous fashion, but I am sure he would have chosen a lady of merit. He imagined her to be such no doubt, and drew a charming picture of her occupations by the banks of the river; but in his other imaginations, there was some kind of peg on which to hang the false costumes he created; windmills are big, and wave their arms like giants; sheep in the distance are somewhat like an army; a little boat on the riverside must look much the same whether enchanted or belonging to millers; but except that Dulcinea is a woman, she bears no resemblance at all to the damsel of his imagination.'

At the time of these letters, the oldest son only was born to them. In September of the next year, with the birth of the second, Charles Frewen, there befell Fleeming a terrible alarm and what proved to be a lifelong misfortune. Mrs. Jenkin was taken suddenly and alarmingly ill; Fleeming ran a matter of two miles to fetch the doctor, and, drenched with sweat as he was, returned with him at once in an open gig. On their arrival at the house, Mrs. Jenkin half unconsciously took and kept hold of her husband's hand. By the doctor's orders, windows and doors were set open to create a thorough draught, and the patient was on no account to be disturbed. Thus, then, did Fleeming pass the whole of that night, crouching on the floor in the draught, and not daring to move lest he should wake the sleeper. He had never been strong; energy had stood him instead of vigour; and the result of that night's exposure was flying rheumatism varied by settled sciatica. Sometimes it quite disabled him, sometimes it was less acute; but he was rarely free from it until his death. I knew him for many years; for more than ten we were closely intimate; I have lived with him for weeks; and during all this time, he only once referred to his infirmity and then perforce as an excuse for some trouble he put me to, and so slightly worded that I paid no heed. This is a good measure of his courage under sufferings of which none but the untried will think lightly. And I think it worth noting how this optimist was acquainted with pain. It will seem strange only to the superficial. The disease of pessimism springs never from real troubles, which it braces men to bear, which it delights men to bear well. Nor does it readily spring at all, in minds that have conceived of life as a field of ordered duties, not as a chase in which to hunt for gratifications. 'We are not here to be happy, but to be good'; I wish he had mended the phrase: 'We are not here to be happy, but to try to be good,' comes nearer the modesty of truth. With such old-fashioned morality, it is possible to get through life, and see the worst of it, and feel some of the worst of it, and still acquiesce piously and even gladly in man's fate. Feel some of the worst of it, I say; for some of the rest of the worst is, by this simple faith, excluded.

It was in the year 1868, that the clouds finally rose. The business in partnership with Mr. Forde began suddenly to pay well; about the same time the patents showed themselves a valuable property; and but a little after, Fleeming was appointed to the new chair of engineering in the University of Edinburgh. Thus, almost at once, pecuniary embarrassments passed for ever out of his life. Here is his own epilogue to the time at Claygate, and his anticipations of the future in Edinburgh.

'.... The dear old house at Claygate is not let and the pretty garden a mass of weeds. I feel rather as if we had behaved unkindly to them. We were very happy there, but now that it is over I am conscious of the weight of anxiety as to money which I bore all the time. With you in the garden, with Austin in the coach-house, with pretty songs in the little, low white room, with the moonlight in the dear room up-stairs, ah, it was perfect; but the long walk, wondering, pondering, fearing, scheming, and the dusty jolting railway, and the horrid fusty office with its endless disappointments, they are well gone. It is well enough to fight and scheme and bustle about in the eager crowd here [in London] for a while now and then, but not for a lifetime. What I have now is just perfect. Study for winter, action for summer, lovely country for recreation, a pleasant town for talk...'

CHAPTER V. - NOTES OF TELEGRAPH VOYAGES, 1858 TO 1873.

BUT it is now time to see Jenkin at his life's work. I have before me certain imperfect series of letters written, as he says, 'at hazard, for one does not know at the time what is important and what is not': the earlier addressed to Miss Austin, after the betrothal; the later to Mrs. Jenkin the young wife. I should premise that I have allowed myself certain editorial freedoms, leaving out and splicing together much as he himself did with the Bona cable: thus edited the letters speak for themselves, and will fail to interest none who love adventure or activity. Addressed as they were to her whom he called his 'dear engineering pupil,' they give a picture of his work so clear that a child may understand, and so attractive that I am half afraid their publication may prove harmful, and still further crowd the ranks of a profession already overcrowded. But their most engaging quality is the picture of the writer; with his indomitable self-confidence and courage, his readiness in every pinch of circumstance or change of plan, and his ever fresh enjoyment of the whole web of human experience, nature, adventure, science, toil and rest, society and solitude. It should be borne in mind that the writer of these buoyant pages was, even while he wrote, harassed by responsibility, stinted in sleep and often struggling with the prostration of sea-sickness. To this last enemy, which he never overcame, I have omitted, in my search after condensation, a good many references; if they were all left, such was the man's temper, they would not represent one hundredth part of what he suffered, for he was never given to complaint. But indeed he had met this ugly trifle, as he met every thwart circumstance of life, with a certain pleasure of pugnacity; and suffered it not to check him, whether in the exercise of his profession or the pursuit of amusement.

I.

'Birkenhead: April 18, 1858.

'Well, you should know, Mr. - having a contract to lay down a submarine telegraph from Sardinia to Africa failed three times in the attempt. The distance from land to land is about 140 miles. On the first occasion, after proceeding some 70 miles, he had to cut the cable - the cause I forget; he tried again, same result; then picked up about 20 miles of the lost cable, spliced on a new piece, and very nearly got across that time, but ran short of cable, and when but a few miles off Galita in very deep water, had to telegraph to London for more cable to be manufactured and sent out whilst he tried to stick to the end: for five days, I think, he lay there sending and receiving messages, but heavy weather coming on the cable parted and Mr. - went home in despair - at least I should think so.

'He then applied to those eminent engineers, R. S. Newall & Co., who made and laid down a cable for him last autumn - Fleeming Jenkin (at the time in considerable mental agitation) having the honour of fitting out the ELBA for that purpose.' [On this occasion, the ELBA has no cable to lay; but] 'is going out in the beginning of May to endeavour to fish up the cables Mr. - lost. There are two ends at or near the shore: the third will probably not be found within 20 miles from land. One of these ends will be passed over a very big pulley or sheave at the bows, passed six times round a big barrel or drum; which will be turned round by a steam engine on deck, and thus wind up the cable, while the ELBA slowly steams ahead. The cable is not wound round and round the drum as your silk is wound on its reel, but on the contrary never goes round more than six times, going off at one side as it comes on at the other, and going down into the hold of the ELBA to be coiled along in a big coil or skein.

'I went down to Gateshead to discuss with Mr. Newall the form which this tolerably simple idea should take, and have been busy since I came here drawing, ordering, and putting up the machinery - uninterfered with, thank goodness, by any one. I own I like responsibility; it flatters one and then, your father might say, I have more to gain than to lose. Moreover I do like this bloodless, painless combat with wood and iron, forcing the stubborn rascals to do my will, licking the clumsy cubs into an active shape, seeing the child of to-day's thought working to-morrow in full vigour at his appointed task.

'May 12.

'By dint of bribing, bullying, cajoling, and going day by day to see the state of things ordered, all my work is very nearly ready now; but those who have neglected these precautions are of course disappointed. Five hundred fathoms of chain [were] ordered by - some three weeks since, to be ready by the 10th without fail; he sends for it to-day - 150 fathoms all they can let us have by the 15th - and how the rest is to be got, who knows? He ordered a boat a month since and yesterday we could see nothing of her but the keel and about two planks. I could multiply instances without end. At first one goes nearly mad with vexation at these things; but one finds so soon that they are the rule, that then it becomes necessary to feign a rage one does not feel. I look upon it as the natural order of things, that if I order a thing, it will not be done - if by accident it gets done, it will certainly be done wrong: the only remedy being to watch the performance at every stage.

'To-day was a grand field-day. I had steam up and tried the engine against pressure or resistance. One part of the machinery is driven by a belt or strap of leather. I always had my doubts this might slip; and so it did, wildly. I had made provision for doubling it, putting on two belts instead of one. No use - off they went, slipping round and off the pulleys instead of driving the machinery. Tighten them - no use. More strength there - down with the lever - smash something, tear the belts, but get them tight - now then, stand clear, on with the steam; - and the belts slip away as if nothing held them. Men begin to look queer; the circle of quidnuncs make sage remarks. Once more - no use. I begin to know I ought to feel sheepish and beat, but somehow I feel cocky instead. I laugh and say, "Well, I am bound to break something down" - and suddenly see. "Oho, there's the place; get weight on there, and the belt won't slip." With much labour, on go the belts again. "Now then, a spar thro' there and six men's weight on; mind you're not carried away." - "Ay, ay, sir." But evidently no one believes in the plan. "Hurrah, round she goes - stick to your spar. All right, shut off steam." And the difficulty is vanquished.

'This or such as this (not always quite so bad) occurs hour after hour, while five hundred tons of coal are rattling down into the holds and bunkers, riveters are making their infernal row all round, and riggers bend the sails and fit the rigging:- a sort of Pandemonium, it appeared to young Mrs. Newall, who was here on Monday and half-choked with guano; but it suits the likes o' me.

'S. S. ELBA, River Mersey: May 17.

'We are delayed in the river by some of the ship's papers not being ready. Such a scene at the dock gates. Not a sailor will join till the last moment; and then, just as the ship forges ahead through the narrow pass, beds and baggage fly on board, the men half tipsy clutch at the rigging, the captain swears, the women scream and sob, the crowd cheer and laugh, while one or two pretty little girls stand still and cry outright, regardless of all eyes.

'These two days of comparative peace have quite set me on my legs again. I was getting worn and weary with anxiety and work. As usual I have been delighted with my shipwrights. I gave them some beer on Saturday, making a short oration. To-day when they went ashore and I came on board, they gave three cheers, whether for me or the ship I hardly know, but I had just bid them good-bye, and the ship was out of hail; but I was startled and hardly liked to claim the compliment by acknowledging it.

'S. S. ELBA: May 25.

'My first intentions of a long journal have been fairly frustrated by sea-sickness. On Tuesday last about noon we started from the Mersey in very dirty weather, and were hardly out of the river when we met a gale from the south-west and a heavy sea, both right in our teeth; and the poor ELBA had a sad shaking. Had I not been very sea-sick, the sight would have been exciting enough, as I sat wrapped in my oilskins on the bridge; [but] in spite of all my efforts to talk, to eat, and to grin, I soon collapsed into imbecility; and I was heartily thankful towards evening to find myself in bed.

'Next morning, I fancied it grew quieter and, as I listened, heard, "Let go the anchor," whereon I concluded we had run into Holyhead Harbour, as was indeed the case. All that day we lay in Holyhead, but I could neither read nor write nor draw. The captain of another steamer which had put in came on board, and we all went for a walk on the hill; and in the evening there was an exchange of presents. We gave some tobacco I think, and received a cat, two pounds of fresh butter, a Cumberland ham, WESTWARD HO! and Thackeray's ENGLISH HUMOURISTS. I was astonished at receiving two such fair books from the captain of a little coasting screw. Our captain said he [the captain of the screw] had plenty of money, five or six hundred a year at least. - "What in the world makes him go rolling about in such a craft, then?" - "Why, I fancy he's reckless; he's desperate in love with that girl I mentioned, and she won't look at him." Our honest, fat, old captain says this very grimly in his thick, broad voice.

'My head won't stand much writing yet, so I will run up and take a look at the blue night sky off the coast of Portugal.

'May 26.

'A nice lad of some two and twenty, A- by name, goes out in a nondescript capacity as part purser, part telegraph clerk, part generally useful person. A- was a great comfort during the miseries [of the gale]; for when with a dead head wind and a heavy sea, plates, books, papers, stomachs were being rolled about in sad confusion, we generally managed to lie on our backs, and grin, and try discordant staves of the FLOWERS OF THE FOREST and the LOW-BACKED CAR. We could sing and laugh, when we could do nothing else; though A- was ready to swear after each fit was past, that that was the first time he had felt anything, and at this moment would declare in broad Scotch that he'd never been sick at all, qualifying the oath with "except for a minute now and then." He brought a cornet-a-piston to practice on, having had three weeks' instructions on that melodious instrument; and if you could hear the horrid sounds that come! especially at heavy rolls. When I hint he is not improving, there comes a confession: "I don't feel quite right yet, you see!" But he blows away manfully, and in self-defence I try to roar the tune louder.

'11:30 P.M.

'Long past Cape St. Vincent now. We went within about 400 yards of the cliffs and light-house in a calm moonlight, with porpoises springing from the sea, the men crooning long ballads as they lay idle on the forecastle and the sails flapping uncertain on the yards. As we passed, there came a sudden breeze from land, hot and heavy scented; and now as I write its warm rich flavour contrasts strongly with the salt air we have been breathing.

'I paced the deck with H-, the second mate, and in the quiet night drew a confession that he was engaged to be married, and gave him a world of good advice. He is a very nice, active, little fellow, with a broad Scotch tongue and "dirty, little rascal" appearance. He had a sad disappointment at starting. Having been second mate on the last voyage, when the first mate was discharged, he took charge of the ELBA all the time she was in port, and of course looked forward to being chief mate this trip. Liddell promised him the post. He had not authority to do this; and when Newall heard of it, he appointed another man. Fancy poor H-having told all the men and most of all, his sweetheart. But more remains behind; for when it came to signing articles, it turned out that O-, the new first mate, had not a certificate which allowed him to have a second mate. Then came rather an affecting scene. For H- proposed to sign as chief (he having the necessary higher certificate) but to act as second for the lower wages. At first O- would not give in, but offered to go as second. But our brave little H- said, no: "The owners wished Mr. O- to be chief mate, and chief mate he should be." So he carried the day, signed as chief and acts as second. Shakespeare and Byron are his favourite books. I walked into Byron a little, but can well understand his stirring up a rough, young sailor's romance. I lent him WESTWARD HO from the cabin; but to my astonishment he did not care much for it; he said it smelt of the shilling railway library; perhaps I had praised it too highly. Scott is his standard for novels. I am very happy to find good taste by no means confined to gentlemen, H- having no pretensions to that title. He is a man after my own heart.

'Then I came down to the cabin and heard young A-'s

schemes for the future. His highest picture is a commission in the Prince of Vizianagram's irregular horse. His eldest brother is tutor to his Highness's children, and grand vizier, and magistrate, and on his Highness's household staff, and seems to be one of those Scotch adventurers one meets with and hears of in queer berths - raising cavalry, building palaces, and using some petty Eastern king's long purse with their long Scotch heads.

'Off Bona; June 4.

'I read your letter carefully, leaning back in a Maltese boat to present the smallest surface of my body to a grilling sun, and sailing from the ELBA to Cape Hamrah about three miles distant. How we fried and sighed! At last, we reached land under Fort Genova, and I was carried ashore pick-a-back, and plucked the first flower I saw for Annie. It was a strange scene, far more novel than I had imagined: the high, steep banks covered with rich, spicy vegetation of which I hardly knew one plant. The dwarf palm with fan-like leaves, growing about two feet high, formed the staple of the verdure. As we brushed through them, the gummy leaves of a cistus stuck to the clothes; and with its small white flower and yellow heart, stood for our English dog-rose. In place of heather, we had myrtle and lentisque with leaves somewhat similar. That large bulb with long flat leaves? Do not touch it if your hands are cut; the Arabs use it as blisters for their horses. Is that the same sort? No, take that one up; it is the bulb of a dwarf palm, each layer of the onion peels off, brown and netted, like the outside of a cocoa-nut. It is a clever plant that; from the leaves we get a vegetable horsehair; - and eat the bottom of the centre spike. All the leaves you pull have the same aromatic scent. But here a little patch of cleared ground shows old friends, who seem to cling by abused civilisation:- fine, hardy thistles, one of them bright yellow, though; - honest, Scotch-looking, large daisies or gowans; - potatoes here and there, looking but sickly; and dark sturdy fig-trees looking cool and at their ease in the burning sun.

'Here we are at Fort Genova, crowning the little point, a small old building, due to my old Genoese acquaintance who fought and traded bravely once upon a time. A broken cannon of theirs forms the threshold; and through a dark, low arch, we enter upon broad terraces sloping to the centre, from which rain water may collect and run into that well. Large-breeched French troopers lounge about and are most civil; and the whole party sit down to breakfast in a little white-washed room, from the door of which the long, mountain coastline and the sparkling sea show of an impossible blue through the openings of a white-washed rampart. I try a sea-egg, one of those prickly fellows - sea-urchins, they are called sometimes; the shell is of a lovely purple, and when opened, there are rays of yellow adhering to the inside; these I eat, but they are very fishy.

'We are silent and shy of one another, and soon go out to watch while turbaned, blue-breeched, barelegged Arabs dig holes for the land telegraph posts on the following principle: one man takes a pick and bangs lazily at the hard earth; when a little is loosened, his mate with a small spade lifts it on one side; and DA CAPO. They have regular features and look quite in place among the palms. Our English workmen screw the earthenware insulators on the posts, strain the wire, and order Arabs about by the generic term of Johnny. I find W- has nothing for me to do; and that in fact no one has anything to do. Some instruments for testing have stuck at Lyons, some at Cagliari; and nothing can be done - or at any rate, is done. I wander about, thinking of you and staring at big, green grasshoppers - locusts, some people call them - and smelling the rich brushwood. There was nothing for a pencil to sketch, and I soon got tired of this work, though I have paid willingly much money for far less strange and lovely sights.

'Off Cape Spartivento: June 8.

'At two this morning, we left Cagliari; at five cast anchor here. I got up and began preparing for the final trial; and shortly afterwards everyone else of note on board went ashore to make experiments on the state of the cable, leaving me with the prospect of beginning to lift at 12 o'clock. I was not ready by that time; but the experiments were not concluded and moreover the cable was found to be imbedded some four or five feet in sand, so that the boat could not bring off the end. At three, Messrs. Liddell, &c., came on board in good spirits, having found two wires good or in such a state as permitted messages to be transmitted freely. The boat now went to grapple for the cable some way from shore while the ELBA towed a small lateen craft which was to take back the consul to Cagliari some distance on its way. On our return we found the boat had been unsuccessful; she was allowed to drop astern, while we grappled for the cable in the ELBA [without more success]. The coast is a low mountain range covered with brushwood or heather - pools of water and a sandy beach at their feet. I have not yet been ashore, my hands having been very full all day.

'June 9.

'Grappling for the cable outside the bank had been voted too uncertain; [and the day was spent in] efforts to pull the cable off through the sand which has accumulated over it. By getting the cable tight on to the boat, and letting the swell pitch her about till it got slack, and then tightening again with blocks and pulleys, we managed to get out from the beach towards the ship at the rate of about twenty yards an hour. When they had got about 100 yards from shore, we ran round in the ELBA to try and help them, letting go the anchor in the shallowest possible water, this was about sunset. Suddenly someone calls out he sees the cable at the bottom: there it was sure enough, apparently wriggling about as the waves rippled. Great excitement; still greater when we find our own anchor is foul of it and has been the means of bringing it to light. We let go a grapnel, get the cable clear of the anchor on to the grapnel - the captain in an agony lest we should drift ashore meanwhile - hand the grappling line into the big boat, steam out far enough, and anchor again. A little more work and one end of the cable is up over the bows round my drum. I go to my engine and we start hauling in. All goes pretty well, but it is quite dark. Lamps are got at last, and men arranged. We go on for a quarter of a mile or so from shore and then stop at about half-past nine with orders to be up at three. Grand work at last! A number of the SATURDAY REVIEW here; it reads so hot and feverish, so tomblike and unhealthy, in the midst of dear Nature's hills and sea, with good wholesome work to do. Pray that all go well to-morrow.

'June 10.

'Thank heaven for a most fortunate day. At three o'clock this morning in a damp, chill mist all hands were roused to work. With a small delay, for one or two improvements I had seen to be necessary last night, the engine started and since that time I do not think there has been half an hour's stoppage. A rope to splice, a block to change, a wheel to oil, an old rusted anchor to disengage from the cable which brought it up, these have been our only obstructions. Sixty, seventy, eighty, a hundred, a hundred and twenty revolutions at last, my little engine tears away. The even black rope comes straight out of the blue heaving water: passes slowly round an open-hearted, good-tempered looking pulley, five feet diameter; aft past a vicious nipper, to bring all up should anything go wrong; through a gentle guide; on to a huge bluff drum, who wraps him round his body and says "Come you must," as plain as drum can speak: the chattering pauls say "I've got him, I've got him, he can't get back:" whilst black cable, much slacker and easier in mind and body, is taken by a slim V-pulley and passed down into the huge hold, where half a dozen men put him comfortably to bed after his exertion in rising from his long bath. In good sooth, it is one of the strangest sights I know to see that black fellow rising up so steadily in the midst of the blue sea. We are more than half way to the place where we expect the fault; and already the one wire, supposed previously to be quite bad near the African coast, can be spoken through. I am very glad I am here, for my machines are my own children and I look on their little failings with a parent's eye and lead them into the path of duty with gentleness and firmness. I am naturally in good spirits, but keep very quiet, for misfortunes may arise at any instant; moreover to-morrow my paying-out apparatus will be wanted should all go well, and that will be another nervous operation. Fifteen miles are safely in; but no one knows better than I do that nothing is done till all is done.

'June 11.

'9 A.M. - We have reached the splice supposed to be faulty, and no fault has been found. The two men learned in electricity, L- and W-, squabble where the fault is.

'EVENING. - A weary day in a hot broiling sun; no air. After the experiments, L- said the fault might be ten miles ahead: by that time, we should be according to a chart in about a thousand fathoms of water - rather more than a mile. It was most difficult to decide whether to go on or not. I made preparations for a heavy pull, set small things to rights and went to sleep. About four in the afternoon, Mr. Liddell decided to proceed, and we are now (at seven) grinding it in at the rate of a mile and three-quarters per hour, which appears a grand speed to us. If the paying-out only works well! I have just thought of a great improvement in it; I can't apply it this time, however. - The sea is of an oily calm, and a perfect fleet of brigs and ships surrounds us, their sails hardly filling in the lazy breeze. The sun sets behind the dim coast of the Isola San Pietro, the coast of Sardinia high and rugged becomes softer and softer in the distance, while to the westward still the isolated rock of Toro springs from the horizon. - It would amuse you to see how cool (in head) and jolly everybody is. A testy word now and then shows the wires are strained a little, but everyone laughs and makes his little jokes as if it were all in fun:

yet we are all as much in earnest as the most earnest of the earnest bastard German school or demonstrative of Frenchmen. I enjoy it very much.

'June 12.

'5.30 A.M. - Out of sight of land: about thirty nautical miles in the hold; the wind rising a little; experiments being made for a fault, while the engine slowly revolves to keep us hanging at the same spot: depth supposed about a mile. The machinery has behaved admirably. Oh! that the paying-out were over! The new machinery there is but rough, meant for an experiment in shallow water, and here we are in a mile of water.

'6.30. - I have made my calculations and find the new paying-out gear cannot possibly answer at this depth, some portion would give way. Luckily, I have brought the old things with me and am getting them rigged up as fast as may be. Bad news from the cable. Number four has given in some portion of the last ten miles: the fault in number three is still at the bottom of the sea: number two is now the only good wire and the hold is getting in such a mess, through keeping bad bits out and cutting for splicing and testing, that there will be great risk in paying out. The cable is somewhat strained in its ascent from one mile below us; what it will be when we get to two miles is a problem we may have to determine.

'9 P.M. - A most provoking unsatisfactory day. We have done nothing. The wind and sea have both risen. Too little notice has been given to the telegraphists who accompany this expedition; they had to leave all their instruments at Lyons in order to arrive at Bona in time; our tests are therefore of the roughest, and no one really knows where the faults are. Mr. L- in the morning lost much time; then he told us, after we had been inactive for about eight hours, that the fault in number three was within six miles; and at six o'clock in the evening, when all was ready for a start to pick up these six miles, he comes and says there must be a fault about thirty miles from Bona! By this time it was too late to begin paying out today, and we must lie here moored in a thousand fathoms till light to-morrow morning. The ship pitches a good deal, but the wind is going down.

'June 13, Sunday.

'The wind has not gone down, however. It now (at 10.30) blows a pretty stiff gale, the sea has also risen; and the ELBA'S bows rise and fall about 9 feet. We make twelve pitches to the minute, and the poor cable must feel very sea-sick by this time. We are quite unable to do anything, and continue riding at anchor in one thousand fathoms, the engines going constantly so as to keep the ship's bows up to the cable, which by this means hangs nearly vertical and sustains no strain but that caused by its own weight and the pitching of the vessel. We were all up at four, but the weather entirely forbade work for to-day, so some went to bed and most lay down, making up our leeway as we nautically term our loss of sleep. I must say Liddell is a fine fellow and keeps his patience and temper wonderfully; and yet how he does fret and fume about trifles at home! This wind has blown now for 36 hours, and yet we have telegrams from Bona to say the sea there is as calm as a mirror. It makes one laugh to remember one is still tied to the shore. Click, click, click, the pecker is at work: I wonder what Herr P - says to Herr L -, - tests, tests, tests, nothing more.

This will be a very anxious day.

'June 14.

'Another day of fatal inaction.

'June 15.

'9.30. - The wind has gone down a deal; but even now there are doubts whether we shall start to-day. When shall I get back to you?

'9 P.M. - Four miles from land. Our run has been successful and eventless. Now the work is nearly over I feel a little out of spirits - why, I should be puzzled to say - mere wantonness, or reaction perhaps after suspense.

'June 16.

'Up this morning at three, coupled my self-acting gear to the brake and had the satisfaction of seeing it pay out the last four miles in very good style. With one or two little improvements, I hope to make it a capital thing. The end has just gone ashore in two boats, three out of four wires good. Thus ends our first expedition. By some odd chance a TIMES of June the 7th has found its way on board through the agency of a wretched old peasant who watches the end of the line here. A long account of breakages in the Atlantic trial trip. To-night we grapple for the heavy cable, eight tons to the mile. I long to have a tug at him; he may puzzle me, and though misfortunes or rather difficulties are a bore at the time, life when working with cables is tame without them.

'2 P.M. - Hurrah, he is hooked, the big fellow, almost at the first cast. He hangs under our bows looking so huge and imposing that I could find it in my heart to be afraid of him.

'June 17.

'We went to a little bay called Chia, where a freshwater stream falls into the sea, and took in water. This is rather a long operation, so I went a walk up the valley with Mr. Liddell. The coast here consists of rocky mountains 800 to 1,000 feet high covered with shrubs of a brilliant green. On landing our first amusement was watching the hundreds of large fish who lazily swam in shoals about the river; the big canes on the further side hold numberless tortoises, we are told, but see none, for just now they prefer taking a siesta. A little further on, and what is this with large pink flowers in such abundance? - the oleander in full flower. At first I fear to pluck them, thinking they must be cultivated and valuable; but soon the banks show a long line of thick tall shrubs, one mass of glorious pink and green. Set these in a little valley, framed by mountains whose rocks gleam out blue and purple colours such as pre-Raphaelites only dare attempt, shining out hard and weird-like amongst the clumps of castor-oil plants, oistus, arbor vitae and many other evergreens, whose names, alas! I know not; the cistus is brown now, the rest all deep or brilliant green. Large herds of cattle browse on the baked deposit at the foot of these large crags. One or two half-savage herdsmen in sheepskin kilts, &c., ask for cigars; partridges whirr up on either side of us; pigeons coo and nightingales sing amongst the blooming oleander. We get six sheep and many fowls, too, from the priest of the small village; and then run back to Spartivento and make preparations for the morning.

'June 18.

'The big cable is stubborn and will not behave like his smaller brother. The gear employed to take him off the drum is not strong enough; he gets slack on the drum and plays the mischief. Luckily for my own conscience, the gear I had wanted was negatived by Mr. Newall. Mr. Liddell does not exactly blame me, but he says we might have had a silver pulley cheaper than the cost of this delay. He has telegraphed for more men to Cagliari, to try to pull the cable off the drum into the hold, by hand. I look as comfortable as I can, but feel as if people were blaming me. I am trying my best to get something rigged which may help us; I wanted a little difficulty, and feel much better. - The short length we have picked up was covered at places with beautiful sprays of coral, twisted and twined with shells of those small, fairy animals we saw in the aquarium at home; poor little things, they died at once, with their little bells and delicate bright tints.

'12 O'CLOCK. - Hurrah, victory! for the present anyhow. Whilst in our first dejection, I thought I saw a place where a flat roller would remedy the whole misfortune; but a flat roller at Cape Spartivento, hard, easily unshipped, running freely! There was a grooved pulley used for the paying-out machinery with a spindle wheel, which might suit me. I filled him up with tarry spunyarn, nailed sheet copper round him, bent some parts in the fire; and we are paying-in without more trouble now. You would think some one would praise me; no, no more praise than blame before; perhaps now they think better of me, though.

'10 P.M. - We have gone on very comfortably for nearly six miles. An hour and a half was spent washing down; for along with many coloured polypi, from corals, shells and insects, the big cable brings up much mud and rust, and makes a fishy smell by no means pleasant: the bottom seems to teem with life. - But now we are startled by a most unpleasant, grinding noise; which appeared at first to come from the large low pulley, but when the engines stopped, the noise continued; and we now imagine it is something slipping down the cable, and the pulley but acts as sounding-board to the big fiddle. Whether it is only an anchor or one of the two other cables, we know not. We hope it is not the cable just laid down.

'June 19.

'10 A.M. - All our alarm groundless, it would appear: the odd noise ceased after a time, and there was no mark sufficiently strong on the large cable to warrant the suspicion that we had cut another line through. I stopped up on the look-out till three in the morning, which made 23 hours between sleep and sleep. One goes dozing about, though, most of the day, for it is only when something goes wrong that one has to look alive. Hour after hour, I stand on the forecastle-head, picking off little specimens of polypi and coral, or lie on the saloon deck reading back numbers of the TIMES - till something hitches, and then all is hurly-burly once more. There are awnings all along the ship, and a most ancient, fish-like smell beneath.

'1 O'CLOCK. - Suddenly a great strain in only 95 fathoms of water - belts surging and general dismay; grapnels being thrown out in the hope of finding what holds the cable. - Should it prove the young cable! We are apparently crossing its path - not the working one, but the lost child; Mr. Liddell WOULD start the big one first though it was laid first: he wanted to see the job done, and meant to leave us to the small one unaided by his presence.

'3.30. - Grapnel caught something, lost it again; it left its marks on the prongs. Started lifting gear again; and after hauling in some 50 fathoms - grunt, grunt, grunt - we hear the other cable slipping down our big one, playing the selfsame tune we heard last night - louder, however.

'10 P.M. - The pull on the deck engines became harder and harder. I got steam up in a boiler on deck, and another little engine starts hauling at the grapnel. I wonder if there ever was such a scene of confusion: Mr. Liddell and W- and the captain all giving orders contradictory, &c., on the forecastle; D-, the foreman of our men, the mates, &c., following the example of our superiors; the ship's engine and boilers below, a 50-horse engine on deck, a boiler 14 feet long on deck beside it, a little steam winch tearing round; a dozen Italians (20 have come to relieve our hands, the men we telegraphed for to Cagliari) hauling at the rope; wiremen, sailors, in the crevices left by ropes and machinery; everything that could swear swearing - I found myself swearing like a trooper at last. We got the unknown difficulty within ten fathoms of the surface; but then the forecastle got frightened that, if it was the small cable which we had got hold of, we should certainly break it by continuing the tremendous and increasing strain. So at last Mr. Liddell decided to stop; cut the big cable, buoying its end; go back to our pleasant watering-place at Chia, take more water and start lifting the small cable. The end of the large one has even now regained its sandy bed; and three buoys - one to grapnel foul of the supposed small cable, two to the big cable - are dipping about on the surface. One more - a flag-buoy - will soon follow, and then straight for shore.

'June 20.

'It is an ill-wind, &c. I have an unexpected opportunity of forwarding this engineering letter; for the craft which brought out our Italian sailors must return to Cagliari to-night, as the little cable will take us nearly to Galita, and the Italian skipper could hardly find his way from thence. To-day - Sunday - not much rest. Mr. Liddell is at Spartivento telegraphing. We are at Chia, and shall shortly go to help our boat's crew in getting the small cable on board. We dropped them some time since in order that they might dig it out of the sand as far as possible.

'June 21.

'Yesterday - Sunday as it was - all hands were kept at work all day, coaling, watering, and making a futile attempt to pull the cable from the shore on board through the sand. This attempt was rather silly after the experience we had gained at Cape Spartivento. This morning we grappled, hooked the cable at once, and have made an excellent start. Though I have called this the small cable, it is much larger than the Bona one. - Here comes a break down and a bad one.

'June 22.

'We got over it, however; but it is a warning to me that my future difficulties will arise from parts wearing out.

Yesterday the cable was often a lovely sight, coming out of the water one large incrustation of delicate, net-like corals and long, white curling shells. No portion of the dirty black wires was visible; instead we had a garland of soft pink with little scarlet sprays and white enamel intermixed. All was fragile, however, and could hardly be secured in safety; and inexorable iron crushed the tender leaves to atoms. - This morning at the end of my watch, about 4 o'clock, we came to the buoys, proving our anticipations right concerning the crossing of the cables. I went to bed for four hours, and on getting up, found a sad mess. A tangle of the six-wire cable hung to the grapnel which had been left buoyed, and the small cable had parted and is lost for the present. Our hauling of the other day must have done the mischief.

'June 23.

'We contrived to get the two ends of the large cable and to pick the short end up. The long end, leading us seaward, was next put round the drum and a mile of it picked up; but then, fearing another tangle, the end was cut and buoyed, and we returned to grapple for the three-wire cable. All this is very tiresome for me. The buoying and dredging are managed entirely by W-, who has had much experience in this sort of thing; so I have not enough to do and get very homesick. At noon the wind freshened and the sea rose so high that we had to run for land and are once more this evening anchored at Chia.

'June 24.

'The whole day spent in dredging without success. This operation consists in allowing the ship to drift slowly across the line where you expect the cable to be, while at the end of a long rope, fast either to the bow or stern, a grapnel drags along the ground. This grapnel is a small anchor, made like four pot-hooks tied back to back. When the rope gets taut, the ship is stopped and the grapnel hauled up to the surface in the hopes of finding the cable on its prongs. - I am much discontented with myself for idly lounging about and reading WESTWARD HO! for the second time, instead of taking to electricity or picking up nautical information. I am uncommonly idle. The sea is not quite so rough, but the weather is squally and the rain comes in frequent gusts.

'June 25.

'To-day about 1 o'clock we hooked the three-wire cable, buoyed the long sea end, and picked up the short [or shore] end. Now it is dark and we must wait for morning before lifting the buoy we lowered to-day and proceeding seawards. - The depth of water here is about 600 feet, the height of a respectable English hill; our fishing line was about a quarter of a mile long. It blows pretty fresh, and there is a great deal of sea.

'26th.

'This morning it came on to blow so heavily that it was impossible to take up our buoy. The ELBA recommenced rolling in true Baltic style and towards noon we ran for land.

'27th, Sunday.

'This morning was a beautiful calm. We reached the buoys at about 4.30 and commenced picking up at

6.30. Shortly a new cause of anxiety arose. Kinks came up in great quantities, about thirty in the hour. To have a true conception of a kink, you must see one: it is a loop drawn tight, all the wires get twisted and the gutta-percha inside pushed out. These much diminish the value of the cable, as they must all be cut out, the gutta-percha made good, and the cable spliced. They arise from the cable having been badly laid down so that it forms folds and tails at the bottom of the sea. These kinks have another disadvantage: they weaken the cable very much. - At about six o'clock [P.M.] we had some twelve miles lifted, when I went to the bows; the kinks were exceedingly tight and were giving way in a most alarming manner. I got a cage rigged up to prevent the end (if it broke) from hurting anyone, and sat down on the bowsprit, thinking I should describe kinks to Annie:- suddenly I saw a great many coils and kinks altogether at the surface. I jumped to the gutta-percha pipe, by blowing through which the signal is given to stop the engine. I blow, but the engine does not stop; again - no answer: the coils and kinks jam in the bows and I rush aft shouting stop. Too late: the cable had parted and must lie in peace at the bottom. Someone had pulled the gutta-percha tube across a bare part of the steam pipe and melted it. It had been used hundreds of times in the last few days and gave no symptoms of failing. I believe the cable must have gone at any rate; however, since it went in my watch and since I might have secured the tubing more strongly, I feel rather sad. . . .

'June 28.

'Since I could not go to Annie I took down Shakespeare, and by the time I had finished ANTONY AND CLEOPATRA, read the second half of

TROILUS and got some way in CORIOLANUS, I felt it was childish to regret the accident had happened in my watch, and moreover I felt myself not much to blame in the tubing matter - it had been torn down, it had not fallen down; so I went to bed, and slept without fretting, and woke this morning in the same good mood - for which thank you and our friend Shakespeare. I am happy to say Mr. Liddell said the loss of the cable did not much matter; though this would have been no consolation had I felt myself to blame. - This morning we have grappled for and found another length of small cable which Mr. - dropped in 100 fathoms of water. If this also gets full of kinks, we shall probably have to cut it after 10 miles or so, or more probably still it will part of its own free will or weight.

'10 P.M. - This second length of three-wire cable soon got into the same condition as its fellow - i.e. came up twenty kinks an hour - and after seven miles were in, parted on the pulley over the bows at one of the said kinks; during my watch again, but this time no earthly power could have saved it. I had taken all manner of precautions to prevent the end doing any damage when the smash came, for come I knew it must. We now return to the six-wire cable. As I sat watching the cable to-night, large phosphorescent globes kept rolling from it and fading in the black water.

'29th.

'To-day we returned to the buoy we had left at the end of the six-wire cable, and after much trouble from a series of tangles, got a fair start at noon. You will easily believe a tangle of iron rope inch and a half diameter is not easy to unravel, especially with a ton or so hanging to the ends. It is now eight o'clock and we have about six and a half miles safe: it becomes very exciting, however, for the kinks are coming fast and furious.

'July 2.

'Twenty-eight miles safe in the hold. The ship is now so deep, that the men are to be turned out of their aft hold, and the remainder coiled there; so the good ELBA'S nose need not burrow too far into the waves. There can only be about 10 or 12 miles more, but these weigh 80 or 100 tons.

'July 5.

'Our first mate was much hurt in securing a buoy on the evening of the 2nd. As interpreter [with the Italians] I am useful in all these cases; but for no fortune would I be a doctor to witness these scenes continually. Pain is a terrible thing. - Our work is done: the whole of the six-wire cable has been recovered; only a small part of the three-wire, but that wire was bad and, owing to its twisted state, the value small. We may therefore be said to have been very successful.'

II.

I have given this cruise nearly in full. From the notes, unhappily imperfect, of two others, I will take only specimens; for in all there are features of similarity and it is possible to have too much even of submarine telegraphy and the romance of engineering. And first from the cruise of 1859 in the Greek Islands and to

Alexandria, take a few traits, incidents and pictures.

'May 10, 1859.

'We had a fair wind and we did very well, seeing a little bit of Cerig or Cythera, and lots of turtle-doves wandering about over the sea and perching, tired and timid, in the rigging of our little craft. Then Falconera, Antimilo, and Milo, topped with huge white clouds, barren, deserted, rising bold and mysterious from the blue, chafing sea; - Argentiera, Siphano, Scapho, Paros, Antiparos, and late at night Syra itself. ADAM BEDE in one hand, a sketch-book in the other, lying on rugs under an awning, I enjoyed a very pleasant day.

'May 14.

'Syra is semi-eastern. The pavement, huge shapeless blocks sloping to a central gutter; from this bare two-storied houses, sometimes plaster many coloured, sometimes rough-hewn marble, rise, dirty and ill-finished to straight, plain, flat roofs; shops guiltless of windows, with signs in Greek letters; dogs, Greeks in blue, baggy, Zouave breeches and a fez, a few narghilehs and a sprinkling of the ordinary continental shopboys. - In the evening I tried one more walk in Syra with A-, but in vain endeavoured to amuse myself or to spend money; the first effort resulting in singing DOODAH to a passing Greek or two, the second in spending, no, in making A- spend, threepence on coffee for three.

'May 16.

'On coming on deck, I found we were at anchor in Canea bay, and saw one of the most lovely sights man could witness. Far on either hand stretch bold mountain capes, Spada and Maleka, tender in colour, bold in outline; rich sunny levels lie beneath them, framed by the azure sea. Right in front, a dark brown fortress girdles white mosques and minarets. Rich and green, our mountain capes here join to form a setting for the town, in whose dark walls - still darker - open a dozen high-arched caves in which the huge Venetian galleys used to lie in wait. High above all, higher and higher yet, up into the firmament, range after range of blue and snow-capped mountains. I was bewildered and amazed, having heard nothing of this great beauty. The town when entered is quite eastern. The streets are formed of open stalls under the first story, in which squat tailors, cooks, sherbet vendors and the like, busy at their work or smoking narghilehs. Cloths stretched from house to house keep out the sun. Mules rattle through the crowd; curs yelp between your legs; negroes are as hideous and bright clothed as usual; grave Turks with long chibouques continue to march solemnly without breaking them; a little Arab in one dirty rag pokes fun at two splendid little Turks with brilliant fezzes; wiry mountaineers in dirty, full, white kilts, shouldering long guns and one hand on their pistols, stalk untamed past a dozen Turkish soldiers, who look sheepish and brutal in worn cloth jacket and cotton trousers. A headless, wingless lion of St. Mark still stands upon a gate, and has left the mark of his strong clutch. Of ancient times when Crete was Crete, not a trace remains; save perhaps in the full, well-cut nostril and firm tread of that mountaineer, and I suspect that even his sires were Albanians, mere outer barbarians.

'May 17.

I spent the day at the little station where the cable was landed, which has apparently been first a Venetian monastery and then a Turkish mosque. At any rate the big dome is very cool, and the little ones hold [our electric] batteries capitally. A handsome young Bashibazouk guards it, and a still handsomer mountaineer is the servant; so I draw them and the monastery and the hill, till I'm black in the face with heat and come on board to hear the Canea cable is still bad.

'May 23.

'We arrived in the morning at the east end of Candia, and had a glorious scramble over the mountains which seem built of adamant. Time has worn away the softer portions of the rock, only leaving sharp jagged edges of steel. Sea eagles soaring above our heads; old tanks, ruins, and desolation at our feet. The ancient Arsinoe stood here; a few blocks of marble with the cross attest the presence of Venetian Christians; but now - the desolation of desolations. Mr. Liddell and I separated from the rest, and when we had found a sure bay for the cable, had a tremendous lively scramble back to the boat. These are the bits of our life which I enjoy, which have some poetry, some grandeur in them.

'May 29 (?).

'Yesterday we ran round to the new harbour [of Alexandria], landed the shore end of the cable close to Cleopatra's bath, and made a very satisfactory start about one in the afternoon. We had scarcely gone 200 yards when I noticed that the cable ceased to run out, and I wondered why the ship had stopped. People ran aft to tell me not to put such a strain on the cable; I answered indignantly that there was no strain; and suddenly it broke on every one in the ship at once that we were aground. Here was a nice mess. A violent scirocco blew from the land; making one's skin feel as if it belonged to some one else and didn't fit, making the horizon dim and yellow with fine sand, oppressing every sense and raising the thermometer 20 degrees in an hour, but making calm water round us which enabled the ship to lie for the time in safety. The wind might change at any moment, since the scirocco was only accidental; and at the first wave from seaward bump would go the poor ship, and there would [might] be an end of our voyage. The captain, without waiting to sound, began to make an effort to put the ship over what was supposed to be a sandbank; but by the time soundings were made, this was found to be impossible, and he had only been jamming the poor ELBA faster on a rock. Now every effort was made to get her astern, an anchor taken out, a rope brought to a winch I had for the cable, and the engines backed; but all in vain. A small Turkish Government steamer, which is to be our consort, came to our assistance, but of course very slowly, and much time was occupied before we could get a hawser to her. I could do no good after having made a chart of the soundings round the ship, and went at last on to the bridge to sketch the scene. But at that moment the strain from the winch and a jerk from the Turkish steamer got off the boat, after we had been some hours aground. The carpenter reported that she had made only two inches of water in one compartment; the cable was still uninjured astern, and our spirits rose; when, will you believe it? after going a short distance astern, the pilot ran us once more fast aground on what seemed to me nearly the same spot.

The very same scene was gone through as on the first occasion, and dark came on whilst the wind shifted, and we were still aground. Dinner was served up, but poor Mr. Liddell could eat very little; and bump, bump, grind, grind, went the ship fifteen or sixteen times as we sat at dinner. The slight sea, however, did enable us to bump off. This morning we appear not to have suffered in any way; but a sea is rolling in, which a few hours ago would have settled the poor old ELBA.

'June -.

'The Alexandria cable has again failed; after paying out two-thirds of the distance successfully, an unlucky touch in deep water snapped the line. Luckily the accident occurred in Mr. Liddell's watch. Though personally it may not really concern me, the accident weighs like a personal misfortune. Still I am glad I was present: a failure is probably more instructive than a success; and this experience may enable us to avoid misfortune in still greater undertakings.

'June -.

'We left Syra the morning after our arrival on Saturday the 4th. This we did (first) because we were in a hurry to do something and (second) because, coming from Alexandria, we had four days' quarantine to perform. We were all mustered along the side while the doctor counted us; the letters were popped into a little tin box and taken away to be smoked; the guardians put on board to see that we held no communication with the shore - without them we should still have had four more days' quarantine; and with twelve Greek sailors besides, we started merrily enough picking up the

Canea cable. . . . To our utter dismay, the yarn covering began to come up quite decayed, and the cable, which when laid should have borne half a ton, was now in danger of snapping with a tenth part of that strain. We went as slow as possible in fear of a break at every instant. My watch was from eight to twelve in the morning, and during that time we had barely secured three miles of cable. Once it broke inside the ship, but I seized hold of it in time - the weight being hardly anything - and the line for the nonce was saved. Regular nooses were then planted inboard with men to draw them taut, should the cable break inboard. A-, who should have relieved me, was unwell, so I had to continue my look-out; and about one o'clock the line again parted, but was again caught in the last noose, with about four inches to spare. Five minutes afterwards it again parted and was yet once more caught. Mr. Liddell (whom I had called) could stand this no longer; so we buoyed the line and ran into a bay in Siphano, waiting for calm weather, though I was by no means of opinion that the slight sea and wind had been the cause of our failures. - All next day (Monday) we lay off Siphano, amusing ourselves on shore with fowling pieces and navy revolvers. I need not say we killed nothing; and luckily we did not wound any of ourselves. A guardiano accompanied us, his functions being limited to preventing actual contact with the natives, for they might come as near and talk as much as they pleased. These isles of Greece are sad, interesting places. They are not really barren all over, but they are quite destitute of verdure; and tufts of thyme, wild mastic or mint, though they sound well, are not nearly so pretty as grass. Many little churches, glittering white, dot the islands; most of them, I believe, abandoned during the whole year with the exception of one day sacred to their patron saint. The villages are mean, but the inhabitants do not look wretched and the men are good sailors. There is something in this Greek race yet; they will become a powerful Levantine nation in the course of time. - What a lovely moonlight evening that was! the barren island cutting the clear sky with fantastic outline, marble cliffs on either hand fairly gleaming over the calm sea. Next day, the wind still continuing, I proposed a boating excursion and decoyed A-, L-, and S- into accompanying me. We took the little gig, and sailed away merrily enough round a point to a beautiful white bay, flanked with two glistening little churches, fronted by beautiful distant islands; when suddenly, to my horror, I discovered the ELBA steaming full speed out from the island. Of course we steered after her; but the wind that instant ceased, and we were left in a dead calm. There was nothing for it but to unship the mast, get out the oars and pull. The ship was nearly certain to stop at the buoy; and I wanted to learn how to take an oar, so here was a chance with a vengeance! L- steered, and we three pulled - a broiling pull it was about half way across to Palikandro - still we did come in, pulling an uncommon good stroke, and I had learned to hang on my oar. L- had pressed me to let him take my place; but though I was very tired at the end of the first quarter of an hour, and then every successive half hour, I would not give in. I nearly paid dear for my obstinacy, however; for in the evening I had alternate fits of shivering and burning.'

III.

The next extracts, and I am sorry to say the last, are from Fleeming's letters of 1860, when he was back at

Bona and Spartivento and for the first time at the head of an expedition. Unhappily these letters are not only the last, but the series is quite imperfect; and this is the more to be lamented as he had now begun to use a pen more skilfully, and in the following notes there is at times a touch of real distinction in the manner.

'Cagliari: October 5, 1860.

'All Tuesday I spent examining what was on board the ELBA, and trying to start the repairs of the Spartivento land line, which has been entirely neglected, and no wonder, for no one has been paid for three months, no, not even the poor guards who have to keep themselves, their horses and their families, on their pay. Wednesday morning, I started for Spartivento and got there in time to try a good many experiments. Spartivento looks more wild and savage than ever, but is not without a strange deadly beauty: the hills covered with bushes of a metallic green with coppery patches of soil in between; the valleys filled with dry salt mud and a little stagnant water; where that very morning the deer had drunk, where herons, curlews, and other fowl abound, and where, alas! malaria is breeding with this rain. (No fear for those who do not sleep on shore.) A little iron hut had been placed there since 1858; but the windows had been carried off, the door broken down, the roof pierced all over. In it, we sat to make experiments; and how it recalled Birkenhead! There was Thomson, there was my testing board, the strings of gutta-percha; Harry P- even, battering with the batteries; but where was my darling Annie? Whilst I sat feet in sand, with Harry alone inside the hut -mats, coats, and wood to darken the window - the others visited the murderous old friar, who is of the order of Scaloppi, and for whom I brought a letter from his superior, ordering him to pay us attention; but he was away from home, gone to Cagliari in a boat with the produce of the farm belonging to his convent. Then they visited the tower of Chia, but could not get in because the door is thirty feet off the ground; so they came back and pitched a magnificent tent which I brought from the BAHIANA a long time ago - and where they will live (if I mistake not) in preference to the friar's, or the owl- and bat-haunted tower. MM. T- and S- will be left there: T-, an intelligent, hard-working Frenchman, with whom I am well pleased; he can speak English and Italian well, and has been two years at Genoa. S- is a French German with a face like an ancient Gaul, who has been sergeant-major in the French line and who is, I see, a great, big, muscular FAINEANT. We left the tent pitched and some stores in charge of a guide, and ran back to Cagliari.

'Certainly, being at the head of things is pleasanter than being subordinate. We all agree very well; and I have made the testing office into a kind of private room where I can come and write to you undisturbed, surrounded by my dear, bright brass things which all of them remind me of our nights at Birkenhead. Then I can work here, too, and try lots of experiments; you know how I like that! and now and then I read - Shakespeare principally. Thank you so much for making me bring him: I think I must get a pocket edition of Hamlet and Henry the Fifth, so as never to be without them.

'Cagliari: October 7.

'[The town was full?] . . . of red-shirted English Garibaldini. A very fine looking set of fellows they are, too: the officers rather raffish, but with medals Crimean and Indian; the men a very sturdy set, with many lads of good birth I should say. They still wait their consort the Emperor and will, I fear, be too late to do anything. I meant to have called on them, but they are all gone into barracks some way from the town, and I have been much too busy to go far.

'The view from the ramparts was very strange and beautiful. Cagliari rises on a very steep rock, at the mouth of a wide plain circled by large hills and three-quarters filled with lagoons; it looks, therefore, like an old island citadel. Large heaps of salt mark the border between the sea and the lagoons; thousands of flamingoes whiten the centre of the huge shallow marsh; hawks hover and scream among the trees under the high mouldering battlements. - A little lower down, the band played. Men and ladies bowed and pranced, the costumes posed, church bells tinkled, processions processed, the sun set behind thick clouds capping the hills; I pondered on you and enjoyed it all.

'Decidedly I prefer being master to being man: boats at all hours, stewards flying for marmalade, captain enquiring when ship is to sail, clerks to copy my writing, the boat to steer when we go out - I have run her nose on several times; decidedly, I begin to feel quite a little king. Confound the cable, though! I shall never be able to repair it.

'Bona: October 14.

'We left Cagliari at 4.30 on the 9th and soon got to Spartivento. I repeated some of my experiments, but found Thomson, who was to have been my grand stand-by, would not work on that day in the wretched little hut. Even if the windows and door had been put in, the wind which was very high made the lamp flicker about and blew it out; so I sent on board and got old sails, and fairly wrapped the hut up in them; and then we were as snug as could be, and I left the hut in glorious condition with a nice little stove in it. The tent which should have been forthcoming from the cure's for the guards, had gone to Cagliari; but I found another, [a] green, Turkish tent, in the ELBA and soon had him up. The square tent left on the last occasion was standing all right and tight in spite of wind and rain. We landed provisions, two beds, plates, knives, forks, candles, cooking utensils, and were ready for a start at 6 P.M.; but the wind meanwhile had come on to blow at such a rate that I thought better of it, and we stopped. T- and S- slept ashore, however, to see how they liked it, at least they tried to sleep, for S- the ancient sergeant-major had a toothache, and T- thought the tent was coming down every minute. Next morning they could only complain of sand and a leaky coffee-pot, so I leave them with a good conscience. The little encampment looked quite picturesque: the green round tent, the square white tent and the hut all wrapped up in sails, on a sand hill, looking on the sea and masking those confounded marshes at the back. One would have thought the Cagliaritans were in a conspiracy to frighten the two poor fellows, who (I believe) will be safe enough if they do not go into the marshes after nightfall. S- brought a little dog to amuse them, such a jolly, ugly little cur without a tail, but full of fun; he will be better than quinine.

'The wind drove a barque, which had anchored near us for shelter, out to sea. We started, however, at 2 P.M., and had a quick passage but a very rough one, getting to Bona by daylight [on the 11th]. Such a place as this is for getting anything done! The health boat went away from us at 7.30 with W- on board; and we heard nothing of them till 9.30, when W- came back with two fat Frenchmen who are to look on on the part of the Government. They are exactly alike: only one has four bands and the other three round his cap, and so I know them. Then I sent a boat round to Fort Genois [Fort Genova of 1858], where the cable is landed, with all sorts of things and directions, whilst I went ashore to see about coals and a room at the fort. We hunted people in the little square in their shops and offices, but only found them in cafes. One amiable gentleman wasn't up at 9.30, was out at 10, and as soon as he came back the servant said he would go to bed and not get up till 3: he came, however, to find us at a cafe, and said that, on the contrary, two days in the week he did not do so! Then my two fat friends must have their breakfast after their "something" at a cafe; and all the shops shut from 10 to 2; and the post does not open till 12; and there was a road to Fort Genois, only a bridge had been carried away, &c. At last I got off, and we rowed round to Fort Genois, where my men had put up a capital gipsy tent with sails, and there was my big board and Thomson's number 5 in great glory. I soon came to the conclusion there was a break. Two of my faithful Cagliaritans slept all night in the little tent, to guard it and my precious instruments; and the sea, which was rather rough, silenced my Frenchmen.

'Next day I went on with my experiments, whilst a boat grappled for the cable a little way from shore and buoyed it where the ELBA could get hold. I brought all back to the ELBA, tried my machinery and was all ready for a start next morning. But the wretched coal had not come yet; Government permission from Algiers to be got; lighters, men, baskets, and I know not what forms to be got or got through - and everybody asleep! Coals or no coals, I was determined to start next morning; and start we did at four in the morning, picked up the buoy with our deck engine, popped the cable across a boat, tested the wires to make sure the fault was not behind us, and started picking up at 11. Everything worked admirably, and about 2 P.M., in came the fault. There is no doubt the cable was broken by coral fishers; twice they have had it up to their own knowledge.

'Many men have been ashore to-day and have come back tipsy, and the whole ship is in a state of quarrel from top to bottom, and they will gossip just within my hearing. And we have had, moreover, three French gentlemen and a French lady to dinner, and I had to act host and try to manage the mixtures to their taste. The good-natured little Frenchwoman was most amusing; when I asked her if she would have some apple tart - "MON DIEU," with heroic resignation, "JE VEUX BIEN"; or a little PLOMBODDING - "MAIS CE QUE VOUS VOUDREZ, MONSIEUR!"

'S. S. ELBA, somewhere not far from Bona: Oct. 19.

'Yesterday [after three previous days of useless grappling] was destined to be very eventful. We began dredging at daybreak and hooked at once every time in rocks; but by capital luck, just as we were deciding it was no use to continue in that place, we hooked the cable: up it came, was tested, and lo! another complete break, a quarter of a mile off. I was amazed at my own tranquillity under these disappointments, but I was not really half so fussy as about getting a cab. Well, there was nothing for it but grappling again, and, as you may imagine, we were getting about six miles from shore.

But the water did not deepen rapidly; we seemed to be on the crest of a kind of submarine mountain in prolongation of Cape de Gonde, and pretty havoc we must have made with the crags. What rocks we did hook! No sooner was the grapnel down than the ship was anchored; and then came such a business: ship's engines going, deck engine thundering, belt slipping, fear of breaking ropes: actually breaking grapnels. It was always an hour or more before we could get the grapnel down again. At last we had to give up the place, though we knew we were close to the cable, and go further to sea in much deeper water; to my great fear, as I knew the cable was much eaten away and would stand but little strain. Well, we hooked the cable first dredge this time, and pulled it slowly and gently to the top, with much trepidation. Was it the cable? was there any weight on? it was evidently too small. Imagine my dismay when the cable did come up, but hanging loosely, thus

[Picture]

instead of taut, thus

[Picture]

showing certain signs of a break close by. For a moment I felt provoked, as I thought, "Here we are in deep water, and the cable will not stand lifting!" I tested at once, and by the very first wire found it had broken towards shore and was good towards sea. This was of course very pleasant; but from that time to this, though the wires test very well, not a signal has come from Spartivento. I got the cable into a boat, and a gutta-percha line from the ship to the boat, and we signalled away at a great rate - but no signs of life. The tests, however, make me pretty sure one wire at least is good; so I determined to lay down cable from where we were to the shore, and go to Spartivento to see what had happened there. I fear my men are ill. The night was lovely, perfectly calm; so we lay close to the boat and signals were continually sent, but with no result. This morning I laid the cable down to Fort Genois in style; and now we are picking up odds and ends of cable between the different breaks, and getting our buoys on board, &c. To-morrow I expect to leave for Spartivento.'

IV.

And now I am quite at an end of journal keeping; diaries and diary letters being things of youth which Fleeming had at length outgrown. But one or two more fragments from his correspondence may be taken, and first this brief sketch of the laying of the Norderney cable; mainly interesting as showing under what defects of strength and in what extremities of pain, this cheerful man must at times continue to go about his work.

'I slept on board 29th September having arranged everything to start by daybreak from where we lay in the roads: but at daybreak a heavy mist hung over us so that nothing of land or water could be seen. At midday it lifted suddenly and away we went with perfect weather, but could not find the buoys Forde left, that evening. I saw the captain was not strong in navigation, and took matters next day much more into my own hands and before nine o'clock found the buoys; (the weather had been so fine we had anchored in the open sea near Texel). It took us till the evening to reach the buoys, get the cable on board, test the first half, speak to Lowestoft, make the splice, and start. H- had not finished his work at Norderney, so I was alone on board for Reuter. Moreover the buoys to guide us in our course were not placed, and the captain had very vague ideas about keeping his course; so I had to do a good deal, and only lay down as I was for two hours in the night. I managed to run the course perfectly. Everything went well, and we found Norderney just where we wanted it next afternoon, and if the shore end had been laid, could have finished there and then, October 1st. But when we got to Norderney, we found the CAROLINE with shore end lying apparently aground, and could not understand her signals; so we had to anchor suddenly and I went off in a small boat with the captain to the CAROLINE. It was cold by this time, and my arm was rather stiff and I was tired; I hauled myself up on board the CAROLINE by a rope and found H- and two men on board. All the rest were trying to get the shore end on shore, but had failed and apparently had stuck on shore, and the waves were getting up. We had anchored in the right place and next morning we hoped the shore end would be laid, so we had only to go back. It was of course still colder and quite night. I went to bed and hoped to sleep, but, alas, the rheumatism got into the joints and caused me terrible pain so that I could not sleep. I bore it as long as I could in order to disturb no one, for all were tired; but at last I could bear it no longer and managed to wake the steward and got a mustard poultice which took the pain from the shoulder; but then the elbow got very bad, and I had to call the second steward and get a second poultice, and then it was daylight, and I felt very ill and feverish. The sea was now rather rough - too rough rather for small boats, but luckily a sort of thing called a scoot came out, and we got on board her with some trouble, and got on shore after a good tossing about which made us all sea-sick. The cable sent from the CAROLINE was just 60 yards too short and did not reach the shore, so although the CAROLINE did make the splice late that night, we could neither test nor speak. Reuter was at Norderney, and I had to do the best I could, which was not much, and went to bed early; I thought I should never sleep again, but in sheer desperation got up in the middle of the night and gulped a lot of raw whiskey and slept at last. But not long. A Mr. F- washed my face and hands and dressed me: and we hauled the cable out of the sea, and got it joined to the telegraph station, and on October 3rd telegraphed to Lowestoft first and then to London. Miss Clara Volkman, a niece of Mr. Reuter's, sent the first message to Mrs. Reuter, who was waiting (Varley used Miss Clara's hand as a kind of key), and I sent one of the first messages to Odden. I thought a message addressed to him would not frighten you, and that he would enjoy a message through Papa's cable. I hope he did. They were all very merry, but I had been so lowered by pain that I could not enjoy myself in spite of the success.'

V.

Of the 1869 cruise in the GREAT EASTERN, I give what I am able; only sorry it is no more, for the sake of the ship itself, already almost a legend even to the generation that saw it launched.

'JUNE 17, 1869. - Here are the names of our staff in whom I expect you to be interested, as future GREAT

EASTERN stories may be full of them: Theophilus Smith, a man of Latimer Clark's; Leslie C. Hill, my prizeman at University College; Lord Sackville Cecil; King, one of the Thomsonian Kings; Laws, goes for Willoughby Smith, who will also be on board; Varley, Clark, and Sir James Anderson make up the sum of all you know anything of. A Captain Halpin commands the big ship. There are four smaller vessels. The WM. CORY, which laid the Norderney cable, has already gone to St. Pierre to lay the shore ends. The HAWK and CHILTERN have gone to Brest to lay shore ends. The HAWK and SCANDERIA go with us across the Atlantic and we shall at St. Pierre be transhipped into one or the other.

'JUNE 18. SOMEWHERE IN LONDON. - The shore end is laid, as you may have seen, and we are all under pressing orders to march, so we start from London to-night at 5.10.

'June 20. OFF USHANT. - I am getting quite fond of the big ship. Yesterday morning in the quiet sunlight, she turned so slowly and lazily in the great harbour at Portland, and bye and bye slipped out past the long pier with so little stir, that I could hardly believe we were really off. No men drunk, no women crying, no singing or swearing, no confusion or bustle on deck - nobody apparently aware that they had anything to do. The look of the thing was that the ship had been spoken to civilly and had kindly undertaken to do everything that was necessary without any further interference. I have a nice cabin with plenty of room for my legs in my berth and have slept two nights like a top. Then we have the ladies' cabin set apart as an engineer's office, and I think this decidedly the nicest place in the ship: 35 ft. x 20 ft. broad - four tables, three great mirrors, plenty of air and no heat from the funnels which spoil the great dining-room. I saw a whole library of books on the walls when here last, and this made me less anxious to provide light literature; but alas, to-day I find that they are every one bibles or prayer-books. Now one cannot read many hundred bibles. . . . As for the motion of the ship it is not very much, but 'twill suffice. Thomson shook hands and wished me well. I DO like Thomson. . . . Tell Austin that the GREAT EASTERN has six masts and four funnels. When I get back I will make a little model of her for all the chicks and pay out cotton reels. . . . Here we are at 4.20 at Brest. We leave probably to-morrow morning.

'JULY 12. GREAT EASTERN. - Here as I write we run our last course for the buoy at the St. Pierre shore end. It blows and lightens, and our good ship rolls, and buoys are hard to find; but we must soon now finish our work, and then this letter will start for home. . . . Yesterday we were mournfully groping our way through the wet grey fog, not at all sure where we were, with one consort lost and the other faintly answering the roar of our great whistle through the mist. As to the ship which was to meet us, and pioneer us up the deep channel, we did not know if we should come within twenty miles of her; when suddenly up went the fog, out came the sun, and there, straight ahead, was the WM. CORY, our pioneer, and a little dancing boat, the GULNARE, sending signals of welcome with many-coloured flags. Since then we have been steaming in a grand procession; but now at 2 A.M. the fog has fallen, and the great roaring whistle calls up the distant answering notes all around us. Shall we, or shall we not find the buoy?

'JULY 13. - All yesterday we lay in the damp dripping fog, with whistles all round and guns firing so that we might not bump up against one another. This little delay has let us get our reports into tolerable order. We are now at 7 o'clock getting the cable end again, with the main cable buoy close to us.'

A TELEGRAM OF JULY 20: 'I have received your four welcome letters. The Americans are charming people.'

VI.

And here to make an end are a few random bits about the cruise to Pernambuco:-

'PLYMOUTH, JUNE 21, 1873. - I have been down to the sea-shore and smelt the salt sea and like it; and I have seen the HOOPER pointing her great bow seaward, while light smoke rises from her funnels telling that the fires are being lighted; and sorry as I am to be without you, something inside me answers to the call to be off and doing.

'LALLA ROOKH. PLYMOUTH, JUNE 22. - We have been a little cruise in the yacht over to the Eddystone lighthouse, and my sea-legs seem very well on. Strange how alike all these starts are - first on shore, steaming hot days with a smell of bone-dust and tar and salt water; then the little puffing, panting steam-launch that bustles out across a port with green woody sides, little yachts sliding about, men-of-war training-ships, and then a great big black hulk of a thing with a mass of smaller vessels sticking to it like parasites; and that is one's home being coaled. Then comes the Champagne lunch where everyone says all that is polite to everyone else, and then the uncertainty when to start. So far as we know OW, we are to start tomorrow morning at daybreak; letters that come later are to be sent to Pernambuco by first mail. . . . My father has sent me the heartiest sort of Jack Tar's cheer.

'S. S. HOOPER. OFF FUNCHAL, JUNE 29. - Here we are off Madeira at seven o'clock in the morning. Thomson has been sounding with his special toy ever since half-past three (1087 fathoms of water). I have been watching the day break, and long jagged islands start into being out of the dull night. We are still some miles from land; but the sea is calmer than Loch Eil often was, and the big HOOPER rests very contentedly after a pleasant voyage and favourable breezes. I have not been able to do any real work except the testing [of the cable], for though not sea-sick, I get a little giddy when I try to think on board. . . . The ducks have just had their daily souse and are quacking and gabbling in a mighty way outside the door of the captain's deck cabin where I write. The cocks are crowing, and new-laid eggs are said to be found in the coops. Four mild oxen have been untethered and allowed to walk along the broad iron decks - a whole drove of sheep seem quite content while licking big lumps of bay salt. Two exceedingly impertinent goats lead the cook a perfect life of misery. They steal round the galley and WILL nibble the carrots or turnips if his back is turned for one minute; and then he throws something at them and misses them; and they scuttle off laughing impudently, and flick one ear at him from a safe distance. This is the most impudent gesture I ever saw. Winking is nothing to it. The ear normally hangs down behind; the goat turns sideways to her enemy - by a little knowing cock of the head flicks one ear over one eye, and squints from behind it for half a minute - tosses her head back, skips a pace or two further off, and repeats the manoeuvre. The cook is very fat and cannot run after that goat much.

'PERNAMBUCO, AUG. 1. - We landed here yesterday, all well and cable sound, after a good passage. . . . I am on familiar terms with cocoa-nuts, mangoes, and bread-fruit trees, but I think I like the negresses best of anything I have seen. In turbans and loose sea-green robes, with beautiful black-brown complexions and a stately carriage, they really are a satisfaction to my eye. The weather has been windy and rainy; the HOOPER has to lie about a mile from the town, in an open roadstead, with the whole swell of the Atlantic driving straight on shore. The little steam launch gives all who go in her a good ducking, as she bobs about on the big rollers; and my old gymnastic practice stands me in good stead on boarding and leaving her. We clamber down a rope ladder hanging from the high stern, and then taking a rope in one hand, swing into the launch at the moment when she can contrive to steam up under us - bobbing about like an apple thrown into a tub all the while. The President of the province and his suite tried to come off to a State luncheon on board on Sunday; but the launch being rather heavily laden, behaved worse than usual, and some green seas stove in the President's hat and made him wetter than he had probably ever been in his life; so after one or two rollers, he turned back; and indeed he was wise to do so, for I don't see how he could have got on board. . . . Being fully convinced that the world will not continue to go round unless I pay it personal attention, I must run away to my work.'

CHAPTER VI. - 1869-1885.

Edinburgh - Colleagues - FARRAGO VITAE - I. The Family Circle - Fleeming and his Sons - Highland Life - The Cruise of the Steam Launch - Summer in Styria - Rustic Manners - II. The Drama - Private Theatricals - III. Sanitary Associations - The Phonograph - IV. Fleeming's Acquaintance with a Student - His late Maturity of Mind - Religion and Morality - His Love of Heroism - Taste in Literature - V. His Talk - His late Popularity - Letter from M. Trelat.

THE remaining external incidents of Fleeming's life, pleasures, honours, fresh interests, new friends, are not such as will bear to be told at any length or in the temporal order. And it is now time to lay narration by, and to look at the man he was and the life he lived, more largely.

Edinburgh, which was thenceforth to be his home, is a metropolitan small town; where college professors and the lawyers of the Parliament House give the tone, and persons of leisure, attracted by educational advantages, make up much of the bulk of society. Not, therefore, an unlettered place, yet not pedantic, Edinburgh will compare favourably with much larger cities. A hard and disputatious element has been commented on by strangers: it would not touch Fleeming, who was himself regarded, even in this metropolis of disputation, as a thorny table-mate. To golf unhappily he did not take, and golf is a cardinal virtue in the city of the winds. Nor did he become an archer of the Queen's Body-Guard, which is the Chiltern Hundreds of the distasted golfer. He did not even frequent the Evening Club, where his colleague Tait (in my day) was so punctual and so genial. So that in some ways he stood outside of the lighter and kindlier life of his new home. I should not like to say that he was generally popular; but there as elsewhere, those who knew him well enough to love him, loved him well. And he, upon his side, liked a place where a dinner party was not of necessity unintellectual, and where men stood up to him in argument.

The presence of his old classmate, Tait, was one of his early attractions to the chair; and now that Fleeming is gone again, Tait still remains, ruling and really teaching his great classes. Sir Robert Christison was an old friend of his mother's; Sir Alexander Grant, Kelland, and Sellar, were new acquaintances and highly valued; and these too, all but the last, have been taken from their friends and labours. Death has been busy in the Senatus. I will speak elsewhere of Fleeming's demeanour to his students; and it will be enough to add here that his relations with his colleagues in general were pleasant to himself.

Edinburgh, then, with its society, its university work, its delightful scenery, and its skating in the winter, was thenceforth his base of operations. But he shot meanwhile erratic in many directions: twice to America, as we have seen, on telegraph voyages; continually to London on business; often to Paris; year after year to the Highlands to shoot, to fish, to learn reels and Gaelic, to make the acquaintance and fall in love with the character of Highlanders; and once to Styria, to hunt chamois and dance with peasant maidens. All the while, he was pursuing the course of his electrical studies, making fresh inventions, taking up the phonograph, filled with theories of graphic representation; reading, writing, publishing, founding sanitary associations, interested in technical education, investigating the laws of metre, drawing, acting, directing private theatricals, going a long way to see an actor - a long way to see a picture; in the very bubble of the tideway of contemporary interests. And all the while he was busied about his father and mother, his wife, and in particular his sons; anxiously watching, anxiously guiding these, and plunging with his whole fund of youthfulness into their sports and interests. And all the while he was himself maturing - not in character or body, for these remained young - but in the stocked mind, in the tolerant knowledge of life and man, in pious acceptance of the universe. Here is a farrago for a chapter: here is a world of interests and activities, human, artistic, social, scientific, at each of which he sprang with impetuous pleasure, on each of which he squandered energy, the arrow drawn to the head, the whole intensity of his spirit bent, for the moment, on the momentary purpose. It was this that lent such unusual interest to his society, so that no friend of his can forget that figure of Fleeming coming charged with some new discovery: it is this that makes his character so difficult to represent. Our fathers, upon some difficult theme, would invoke the Muse; I can but appeal to the imagination of the reader. When I dwell upon some one thing, he must bear in mind it was only one of a score; that the unweariable brain was teeming at the very time with other thoughts; that the good heart had left no kind duty forgotten.

I.

In Edinburgh, for a considerable time, Fleeming's family, to three generations, was united: Mr. and Mrs. Austin at Hailes, Captain and Mrs. Jenkin in the suburb of Merchiston, Fleeming himself in the city. It is not every family that could risk with safety such close interdomestic dealings; but in this also Fleeming was particularly favoured. Even the two extremes, Mr. Austin and the Captain, drew together. It is pleasant to find that each of the old gentlemen set a high value on the good looks of the other, doubtless also on his own; and a fine picture they made as they walked the green terrace at Hailes, conversing by the hour. What they talked of is still a mystery to those who knew them; but Mr. Austin always declared that on these occasions he learned much. To both of these families of elders, due service was paid of attention; to both, Fleeming's easy circumstances had brought joy; and the eyes of all were on the grandchildren. In Fleeming's scheme of duties, those of the family stood first; a man was first of all a child, nor did he cease to be so, but only took on added obligations, when he became in turn a father. The care of his parents was always a first thought with him, and their gratification his delight. And the care of his sons, as it was always a grave subject of study with him, and an affair never neglected, so it brought him a thousand satisfactions. 'Hard work they are,' as he once wrote, 'but what fit work!' And again: 'O, it's a cold house where a dog is the only representative of a child!' Not that dogs were despised; we shall drop across the name of Jack, the harum-scarum Irish terrier ere we have done; his own dog Plato went up with him daily to his lectures, and still (like other friends) feels the loss and looks visibly for the reappearance of his master; and Martin, the cat, Fleeming has himself immortalised, to the delight of Mr. Swinburne, in the columns of the SPECTATOR. Indeed there was nothing in which men take interest, in which he took not some; and yet always most in the strong human bonds, ancient as the race and woven of delights and duties.

He was even an anxious father; perhaps that is the part where optimism is hardest tested. He was eager for his sons; eager for their health, whether of mind or body; eager for their education; in that, I should have thought, too eager. But he kept a pleasant face upon all things, believed in play, loved it himself, shared boyishly in theirs, and knew how to put a face of entertainment upon business and a spirit of education into entertainment. If he was to test the progress of the three boys, this advertisement would appear in their little manuscript paper:- 'Notice: The Professor of Engineering in the University of Edinburgh intends at the close of the scholastic year to hold examinations in the following subjects: (1) For boys in the fourth class of the Academy - Geometry and Algebra; (2) For boys at Mr. Henderson's school - Dictation and Recitation; (3) For boys taught exclusively by their mothers - Arithmetic and Reading.' Prizes were given; but what prize would be so conciliatory as this boyish little joke? It may read thin here; it would smack racily in the playroom. Whenever his sons 'started a new fad' (as one of them writes to me) they 'had only to tell him about it, and he was at once interested and keen to help.' He would discourage them in nothing unless it was hopelessly too hard for them; only, if there was any principle of science involved, they must understand the principle; and whatever was attempted, that was to be done thoroughly. If it was but play, if it was but a puppetshow they were to build, he set them the example of being no sluggard in play. When Frewen, the second son, embarked on the ambitious design to make an engine for a toy steamboat, Fleeming made him begin with a proper drawing - doubtless to the disgust of the young engineer; but once that foundation laid, helped in the work with unflagging gusto, 'tinkering away,' for hours, and assisted at the final trial 'in the big bath' with no less excitement than the boy. 'He would take any amount of trouble to help us,' writes my correspondent. 'We never felt an affair was complete till we had called him to see, and he would come at any time, in the middle of any work.' There was indeed one recognised playhour, immediately after the despatch of the day's letters; and the boys were to be seen waiting on the stairs until the mail should be ready and the fun could begin. But at no other time did this busy man suffer his work to interfere with that first duty to his children; and there is a pleasant tale of the inventive Master Frewen, engaged at the time upon a toy crane, bringing to the study where his father sat at work a half-wound reel that formed some part of his design, and observing, 'Papa, you might finiss windin' this for me; I am so very busy to-day.'

I put together here a few brief extracts from Fleeming's letters, none very important in itself, but all together building up a pleasant picture of the father with his sons.

'JAN. 15TH, 1875. - Frewen contemplates suspending soap bubbles by silk threads for experimental purposes. I don't think he will manage that. Bernard' [the youngest] 'volunteered to blow the bubbles with enthusiasm.'

'JAN. 17TH. - I am learning a great deal of electrostatics in consequence of the perpetual cross-examination to which I am subjected. I long for you on many grounds, but one is that I may not be obliged to deliver a running lecture on abstract points of science, subject to cross- examination by two acute students. Bernie does not cross-examine much; but if anyone gets discomfited, he laughs a sort of little silver-whistle giggle, which is trying to the unhappy blunderer.'

'MAY 9TH. - Frewen is deep in parachutes. I beg him not to drop from the top landing in one of his own making.'

'JUNE 6TH, 1876. - Frewen's crank axle is a failure just at present - but he bears up.'

'JUNE 14TH. - The boys enjoy their riding. It gets them whole funds of adventures. One of their caps falling off is matter for delightful reminiscences; and when a horse breaks his step, the occurrence becomes a rear, a shy, or a plunge as they talk it over. Austin, with quiet confidence, speaks of the greater pleasure in riding a spirited horse, even if he does give a little trouble. It is the stolid brute that he dislikes. (N.B. You can still see six inches between him and the saddle when his pony trots.) I listen and sympathise and throw out no hint that their achievements are not really great.'

'JUNE 18TH. - Bernard is much impressed by the fact that I can be useful to Frewen about the steam-boat' [which the latter irrepressible inventor was making]. 'He says quite with awe, "He would not have got on nearly so well if you had not helped him."'

'JUNE 27TH. - I do not see what I could do without Austin. He talks so pleasantly and is so truly good all through.'

'JUNE 27TH. - My chief difficulty with Austin is to get him measured for a pair of trousers. Hitherto I have failed, but I keep a stout heart and mean to succeed. Frewen the observer, in describing the paces of two horses, says, "Polly takes twenty-seven steps to get round the school. I couldn't count Sophy, but she takes more than a hundred."'

'FEB. 18TH, 1877. - We all feel very lonely without you. Frewen had to come up and sit in my room for company last night and I actually kissed him, a thing that has not occurred for years. Jack, poor fellow, bears it as well as he can, and has taken the opportunity of having a fester on his foot, so he is lame and has it bathed, and this occupies his thoughts a good deal.'

'FEB. 19TH. - As to Mill, Austin has not got the list yet. I think it will prejudice him very much against Mill - but that is not my affair. Education of that kind! . . . I would as soon cram my boys with food and boast of the pounds they had eaten, as cram them with literature.'

But if Fleeming was an anxious father, he did not suffer his anxiety to prevent the boys from any manly or even dangerous pursuit. Whatever it might occur to them to try, he would carefully show them how to do it, explain the risks, and then either share the danger himself or, if that were not possible, stand aside and wait the event with that unhappy courage of the looker-on. He was a good swimmer, and taught them to swim. He thoroughly loved all manly exercises; and during their holidays, and principally in the Highlands, helped and encouraged them to excel in as many as possible: to shoot, to fish, to walk, to pull an oar, to hand, reef and steer, and to run a steam launch. In all of these, and in all parts of Highland life, he shared delightedly. He was well onto forty when he took once more to shooting, he was forty-three when he killed his first salmon, but no boy could have more single-mindedly rejoiced in these pursuits. His growing love for the Highland character, perhaps also a sense of the difficulty of the task, led him to take up at forty-one the study of Gaelic; in which he made some shadow of progress, but not much: the fastnesses of that elusive speech retaining to the last their independence. At the house of his friend Mrs. Blackburn, who plays the part of a Highland lady as to the manner born, he learned the delightful custom of kitchen dances, which became the rule at his own house and brought him into yet nearer contact with his neighbours. And thus at forty-two, he began to learn the reel; a study, to which he brought his usual smiling earnestness; and the steps, diagrammatically represented by his own hand, are before me as I write.

It was in 1879 that a new feature was added to the Highland life: a steam launch, called the PURGLE, the Styrian corruption of Walpurga, after a friend to be hereafter mentioned. 'The steam launch goes,' Fleeming wrote. 'I wish you had been present to describe two scenes of which she has been the occasion already: one during which the population of Ullapool, to a baby, was harnessed to her hurrahing - and the other in which the same population sat with its legs over a little pier, watching Frewen and Bernie getting up steam for the first time.' The PURGLE was got with educational intent; and it served its purpose so well, and the boys knew their business so practically, that when the summer was at an end, Fleeming, Mrs. Jenkin, Frewen the engineer, Bernard the stoker, and Kenneth Robertson a Highland seaman, set forth in her to make the passage south. The first morning they got from Loch Broom into Gruinard bay, where they lunched upon an island; but the wind blowing up in the afternoon, with sheets of rain, it was found impossible to beat to sea; and very much in the situation of castaways upon an unknown coast, the party landed at the mouth of Gruinard river. A shooting lodge was spied among the trees; there Fleeming went; and though the master, Mr. Murray, was from home, though the two Jenkin boys were of course as black as colliers, and all the castaways so wetted through that, as they stood in the passage, pools formed about their feet and ran before them into the house, yet Mrs. Murray kindly entertained them for the night. On the morrow, however, visitors were to arrive; there would be no room and, in so out-of-the-way a spot, most probably no food for the crew of the PURGLE; and on the morrow about noon, with the bay white with spindrift and the wind so strong that one could scarcely stand against it, they got up steam and skulked under the land as far as Sanda Bay. Here they crept into a seaside cave, and cooked some food; but the weather now freshening to a gale, it was plain they must moor the launch where she was, and find their way overland to some place of shelter. Even to get their baggage from on board was no light business; for the dingy was blown so far to leeward every trip, that they must carry her back by hand along the beach. But this once managed, and a cart procured in the neighbourhood, they were able to spend the night in a pot-house on Ault Bea. Next day, the sea was unapproachable; but the next they had a pleasant passage to Poolewe, hugging the cliffs, the falling swell bursting close by them in the gullies, and the black scarts that sat like ornaments on the top of every stack and pinnacle, looking down into the PURGLE as she passed. The climate of Scotland had not done with them yet: for three days they lay storm-stayed in Poolewe, and when they put to sea on the morning of the fourth, the sailors prayed them for God's sake not to attempt the passage. Their setting out was indeed merely tentative; but presently they had gone too far to return, and found themselves committed to double Rhu Reay with a foul wind and a cross sea. From half-past eleven in the morning until half-past five at night, they were in immediate and unceasing danger. Upon the least mishap, the PURGLE must either have been swamped by the seas or bulged upon the cliffs of that rude headland. Fleeming and Robertson took turns baling and steering; Mrs. Jenkin, so violent was the commotion of the boat, held on with both hands; Frewen, by Robertson's direction, ran the engine, slacking and pressing her to meet the seas; and Bernard, only twelve years old, deadly sea-sick, and continually thrown against the boiler, so that he was found next day to be covered with burns, yet kept an even fire. It was a very thankful party that sat down that evening to meat in the Hotel at Gairloch. And perhaps, although the thing was new in the family, no one was much surprised when Fleeming said grace over that meal. Thenceforward he continued to observe the form, so that there was kept alive in his house a grateful memory of peril and deliverance. But there was nothing of the muff in Fleeming; he thought it a good thing to escape death, but a becoming and a healthful thing to run the risk of it; and what is rarer, that which he thought for himself, he thought for his family also. In spite of the terrors of Rhu Reay, the cruise was persevered in and brought to an end under happier conditions.

One year, instead of the Highlands, Alt Aussee, in the Steiermark, was chosen for the holidays; and the place, the people, and the life delighted Fleeming. He worked hard at German, which he had much forgotten since he was a boy; and what is highly characteristic, equally hard at the patois, in which he learned to excel. He won a prize at a Schutzen-fest; and though he hunted chamois without much success, brought down more interesting game in the shape of the Styrian peasants, and in particular of his gillie, Joseph. This Joseph was much of a character; and his appreciations of Fleeming have a fine note of their own. The bringing up of the boys he deigned to approve of: 'FAST SO GUT WIE EIN BAUER,' was his trenchant criticism. The attention and courtly respect with which Fleeming surrounded his wife, was something of a puzzle to the philosophic gillie; he announced in the village that Mrs. Jenkin - DIE SILBERNE FRAU, as the folk had prettily named her from some silver ornaments - was a 'GEBORENE GRAFIN' who had married beneath her; and when Fleeming explained what he called the English theory (though indeed it was quite his own) of married relations, Joseph, admiring but unconvinced, avowed it was 'GAR SCHON.' Joseph's cousin, Walpurga Moser, to an orchestra of clarionet and zither, taught the family the country dances, the Steierisch and the Landler, and gained their hearts during the lessons. Her sister Loys, too, who was up at the Alp with the cattle, came down to church on Sundays, made acquaintance with the Jenkins, and must have them up to see the sunrise from her house upon the Loser, where they had supper and all slept in the loft among the hay. The Mosers were not lost sight of; Walpurga still corresponds with Mrs. Jenkin, and it was a late pleasure of Fleeming's to choose and despatch a wedding present for his little mountain friend. This visit was brought to an end by a ball in the big inn parlour; the refreshments chosen, the list of guests drawn up, by Joseph; the best music of the place in attendance; and hosts and guests in their best clothes. The ball was opened by Mrs. Jenkin dancing Steierisch with a lordly Bauer, in gray and silver and with a plumed hat; and Fleeming followed with Walpurga Moser.

There ran a principle through all these holiday pleasures. In Styria as in the Highlands, the same course was followed: Fleeming threw himself as fully as he could into the life and occupations of the native people, studying everywhere their dances and their language, and conforming, always with pleasure, to their rustic etiquette. Just as the ball at Alt Aussee was designed for the taste of Joseph, the parting feast at Attadale was ordered in every particular to the taste of Murdoch the Keeper. Fleeming was not one of the common, so-called gentlemen, who take the tricks of their own coterie to be eternal principles of taste. He was aware, on the other hand, that rustic people dwelling in their own places, follow ancient rules with fastidious precision, and are easily shocked and embarrassed by what (if they used the word) they would have to call the vulgarity of visitors from town. And he, who was so cavalier with men of his own class, was sedulous to shield the more tender feelings of the peasant; he, who could be so trying in a drawing-room, was even punctilious in the cottage. It was in all respects a happy virtue. It renewed his life, during these holidays, in all particulars. It often entertained him with the discovery of strange survivals; as when, by the orders of Murdoch, Mrs. Jenkin must publicly taste of every dish before it was set before her guests. And thus to throw himself into a fresh life and a new school of manners was a grateful exercise of Fleeming's mimetic instinct; and to the pleasures of the open air, of hardships supported, of dexterities improved and displayed, and of plain and elegant society, added a spice of drama.

II.

Fleeming was all his life a lover of the play and all that belonged to it. Dramatic literature he knew fully. He was one of the not very numerous people who can read a play: a knack, the fruit of much knowledge and some imagination, comparable to that of reading score. Few men better understood the artificial principles on which a play is good or bad; few more unaffectedly enjoyed a piece of any merit of construction. His own play was conceived with a double design; for he had long been filled with his theory of the true story of Griselda; used to gird at Father Chaucer for his misconception; and was, perhaps first of all, moved by the desire to do justice to the Marquis of Saluces, and perhaps only in the second place, by the wish to treat a story (as he phrased it) like a sum in arithmetic. I do not think he quite succeeded; but I must own myself no fit judge. Fleeming and I were teacher and taught as to the principles, disputatious rivals in the practice, of dramatic writing.

Acting had always, ever since Rachel and the Marseillaise, a particular power on him. 'If I do not cry at the play,' he used to say, 'I want to have my money back.' Even from a poor play with poor actors, he could draw pleasure. 'Giacometti's ELISABETTA,' I find him writing, 'fetched the house vastly. Poor Queen Elizabeth! And yet it was a little good.' And again, after a night of Salvini: 'I do not suppose any one with feelings could sit out OTHELLO, if Iago and Desdemona were acted.' Salvini was, in his view, the greatest actor he had seen. We were all indeed moved and bettered by the visit of that wonderful man. - 'I declare I feel as if I could pray!' cried one of us, on the return from HAMLET. - 'That is prayer,' said Fleeming. W. B. Hole and I, in a fine enthusiasm of gratitude, determined to draw up an address to Salvini, did so, and carried it to Fleeming; and I shall never forget with what coldness he heard and deleted the eloquence of our draft, nor with what spirit (our vanities once properly mortified) he threw himself into the business of collecting signatures. It was his part, on the ground of his Italian, to see and arrange with the actor; it was mine to write in the ACADEMY a notice of the first performance of MACBETH. Fleeming opened the paper, read so far, and flung it on the floor. 'No,' he cried, 'that won't do. You were thinking of yourself, not of Salvini!' The criticism was shrewd as usual, but it was unfair through ignorance; it was not of myself that I was thinking, but of the difficulties of my trade which I had not well mastered. Another unalloyed dramatic pleasure which Fleeming and I shared the year of the Paris Exposition, was the MARQUIS DE VILLEMER, that blameless play, performed by Madeleine Brohan, Delaunay, Worms, and Broisat - an actress, in such parts at least, to whom I have never seen full justice rendered. He had his fill of weeping on that occasion; and when the piece was at an end, in front of a cafe, in the mild, midnight air, we had our fill of talk about the art of acting.

But what gave the stage so strong a hold on Fleeming was an inheritance from Norwich, from Edward Barron, and from Enfield of the SPEAKER. The theatre was one of Edward Barron's elegant hobbies; he read plays, as became Enfield's son-in-law, with a good discretion; he wrote plays for his family, in which Eliza Barron used to shine in the chief parts; and later in life, after the Norwich home was broken up, his little granddaughter would sit behind him in a great armchair, and be introduced, with his stately elocution, to the world of dramatic literature. From this, in a direct line, we can deduce the charades at Claygate; and after money came, in the Edinburgh days, that private theatre which took up so much of Fleeming's energy and thought. The company - Mr. and Mrs. R. O. Carter of Colwall, W. B. Hole, Captain Charles Douglas, Mr. Kunz, Mr. Burnett, Professor Lewis Campbell, Mr. Charles Baxter, and many more - made a charming society for themselves and gave pleasure to their audience. Mr. Carter in Sir Toby Belch it would be hard to beat. Mr. Hole in broad farce, or as the herald in the TRACHINIAE, showed true stage talent. As for Mrs. Jenkin, it was for her the rest of us existed and were forgiven; her powers were an endless spring of pride and pleasure to her husband; he spent hours hearing and schooling her in private; and when it came to the performance, though there was perhaps no one in the audience more critical, none was more moved than Fleeming. The rest of us did not aspire so high. There were always five performances and weeks of busy rehearsal; and whether we came to sit and stifle as the prompter, to be the dumb (or rather the inarticulate) recipients of Carter's dog whip in the TAMING OF THE SHREW, or having earned our spurs, to lose one more illusion in a leading part, we were always sure at least of a long and an exciting holiday in mirthful company.

In this laborious annual diversion, Fleeming's part was large. I never thought him an actor, but he was something of a mimic, which stood him in stead. Thus he had seen Got in Poirier; and his own Poirier, when he came to play it, breathed meritoriously of the model. The last part I saw him play was Triplet, and at first I thought it promised well. But alas! the boys went for a holiday, missed a train, and were not heard of at home till late at night. Poor Fleeming, the man who never hesitated to give his sons a chisel or a gun, or to send them abroad in a canoe or on a horse, toiled all day at his rehearsal, growing hourly paler, Triplet growing hourly less meritorious. And though the return of the children, none the worse for their little adventure, brought the colour back into his face, it could not restore him to his part. I remember finding him seated on the stairs in some rare moment of quiet during the subsequent performances. 'Hullo, Jenkin,' said I, 'you look down in the mouth.' - 'My dear boy,' said he, 'haven't you heard me? I have not one decent intonation from beginning to end.'

But indeed he never supposed himself an actor; took a part, when he took any, merely for convenience, as one takes a hand at whist; and found his true service and pleasure in the more congenial business of the manager. Augier, Racine, Shakespeare, Aristophanes in Hookham Frere's translation, Sophocles and AEschylus in Lewis Campbell's, such were some of the authors whom he introduced to his public. In putting these upon the stage, he found a thousand exercises for his ingenuity and taste, a thousand problems arising which he delighted to study, a thousand opportunities to make these infinitesimal improvements which are so much in art and for the artist. Our first Greek play had been costumed by the professional costumer, with unforgetable results of comicality and indecorum: the second, the TRACHINIAE, of Sophocles, he took in hand himself, and a delightful task he made of it. His study was then in antiquarian books, where he found confusion, and on statues and bas-reliefs, where he at last found clearness; after an hour or so at the British Museum, he was able to master 'the chiton, sleeves and all'; and before the time was ripe, he had a theory of Greek tailoring at his fingers' ends, and had all the costumes made under his eye as a Greek tailor would have made them. 'The Greeks made the best plays and the best statues, and were the best architects: of course, they were the best tailors, too,' said he; and was never weary, when he could find a tolerant listener, of dwelling on the simplicity, the economy, the elegance both of means and effect, which made their system so delightful.

But there is another side to the stage-manager's employment. The discipline of acting is detestable; the failures and triumphs of that business appeal too directly to the vanity; and even in the course of a careful amateur performance such as ours, much of the smaller side of man will be displayed. Fleeming, among conflicting vanities and levities, played his part to my admiration. He had his own view; he might be wrong; but the performances (he would remind us) were after all his, and he must decide. He was, in this as in all other things, an iron taskmaster, sparing not himself nor others. If you were going to do it at all, he would see that it was done as well as you were able. I have known him to keep two culprits (and one of these his wife) repeating the same action and the same two or three words for a whole weary afternoon. And yet he gained and retained warm feelings from far the most of those who fell under his domination, and particularly (it is pleasant to remember) from the girls. After the slipshod training and the incomplete accomplishments of a girls' school, there was something at first annoying, at last exciting and bracing, in this high standard of accomplishment and perseverance.

III.

It did not matter why he entered upon any study or employment, whether for amusement like the Greek tailoring or the Highland reels, whether from a desire to serve the public as with his sanitary work, or in the view of benefiting poorer men as with his labours for technical education, he 'pitched into it' (as he would have said himself) with the same headlong zest. I give in the Appendix a letter from Colonel Fergusson, which tells fully the nature of the sanitary work and of Fleeming's part and success in it. It will be enough to say here that it was a scheme of protection against the blundering of builders and the dishonesty of plumbers. Started with an eye rather to the houses of the rich, Fleeming hoped his Sanitary Associations would soon extend their sphere of usefulness and improve the dwellings of the poor. In this hope he was disappointed; but in all other ways the scheme exceedingly prospered, associations sprang up and continue to spring up in many quarters, and wherever tried they have been found of use.

Here, then, was a serious employment; it has proved

highly useful to mankind; and it was begun besides, in a mood of bitterness, under the shock of what Fleming would so sensitively feel - the death of a whole family of children. Yet it was gone upon like a holiday jaunt. I read in Colonel Fergusson's letter that his schoolmates bantered him when he began to broach his scheme; so did I at first, and he took the banter as he always did with enjoyment, until he suddenly posed me with the question: 'And now do you see any other jokes to make? Well, then,' said he, 'that's all right. I wanted you to have your fun out first; now we can be serious.' And then with a glowing heat of pleasure, he laid his plans before me, revelling in the details, revelling in hope. It was as he wrote about the joy of electrical experiment. 'What shall I compare them to? A new song? - a Greek play?' Delight attended the exercise of all his powers; delight painted the future. Of these ideal visions, some (as I have said) failed of their fruition. And the illusion was characteristic. Fleming believed we had only to make a virtue cheap and easy, and then all would practise it; that for an end unquestionably good, men would not grudge a little trouble and a little money, though they might stumble at laborious pains and generous sacrifices. He could not believe in any resolute badness. 'I cannot quite say,' he wrote in his young manhood, 'that I think there is no sin or misery. This I can say: I do not remember one single malicious act done to myself. In fact it is rather awkward when I have to say the Lord's Prayer. I have nobody's trespasses to forgive.' And to the point, I remember one of our discussions. I said it was a dangerous error not to admit there were bad people; he, that it was only a confession of blindness on our part, and that we probably called others bad only so far as we were wrapped in ourselves and lacking in the transmigratory forces of imagination. I undertook to describe to him three persons irredeemably bad and whom he should admit to be so. In the first case, he denied my evidence: 'You cannot judge a man upon such testimony,' said he. For the second, he owned it made him sick to hear the tale; but then there was no spark of malice, it was mere weakness I had described, and he had never denied nor thought to set a limit to man's weakness. At my third gentleman, he struck his colours. 'Yes,' said he, 'I'm afraid that is a bad man.' And then looking at me shrewdly: 'I wonder if it isn't a very unfortunate thing for you to have met him.' I showed him radiantly how it was the world we must know, the world as it was, not a world expurgated and prettified with optimistic rainbows. 'Yes, yes,' said he; 'but this badness is such an easy, lazy explanation. Won't you be tempted to use it, instead of trying to understand people?'

In the year 1878, he took a passionate fancy for the phonograph: it was a toy after his heart, a toy that touched the skirts of life, art, and science, a toy prolific of problems and theories. Something fell to be done for a University Cricket Ground Bazaar. 'And the thought struck him,' Mr. Ewing writes to me, 'to exhibit Edison's phonograph, then the very newest scientific marvel. The instrument itself was not to be purchased - I think no specimen had then crossed the Atlantic - but a copy of the TIMES with an account of it was at hand, and by the help of this we made a phonograph which to our great joy talked, and talked, too, with the purest American accent. It was so good that a second instrument was got ready forthwith. Both were shown at the Bazaar: one by Mrs. Jenkin to people willing to pay half a crown for a private view and the privilege of hearing their own voices, while Jenkin, perfervid as usual, gave half-hourly lectures on the other in an adjoining room - I, as his lieutenant, taking turns. The thing was in its way a little triumph. A few of the visitors were deaf, and hugged the belief that they were the victims of a new kind of fancy-fair swindle. Of the others, many who came to scoff remained to take raffle tickets; and one of the phonographs was finally disposed of in this way, falling, by a happy freak of the ballot-box, into the hands of Sir William Thomson.' The other remained in Fleeming's hands, and was a source of infinite occupation. Once it was sent to London, 'to bring back on the tinfoil the tones of a lady distinguished for clear vocalisations; at another time Sir Robert Christison was brought in to contribute his powerful bass'; and there scarcely came a visitor about the house, but he was made the subject of experiment. The visitors, I am afraid, took their parts lightly: Mr. Hole and I, with unscientific laughter, commemorating various shades of Scotch accent, or proposing to 'teach the poor dumb animal to swear.' But Fleeming and Mr. Ewing, when we butterflies were gone, were laboriously ardent. Many thoughts that occupied the later years of my friend were caught from the small utterance of that toy. Thence came his inquiries into the roots of articulate language and the foundations of literary art; his papers on vowel sounds, his papers in the SATURDAY REVIEW upon the laws of verse, and many a strange approximation, many a just note, thrown out in talk and now forgotten. I pass over dozens of his interests, and dwell on this trifling matter of the phonograph, because it seems to me that it depicts the man. So, for Fleeming, one thing joined into another, the greater with the less. He cared not where it was he scratched the surface of the ultimate mystery - in the child's toy, in the great tragedy, in the laws of the tempest, or in the properties of energy or mass - certain that whatever he touched, it was a part of life - and however he touched it, there would flow for his happy constitution interest and delight. 'All fables have their morals,' says Thoreau, 'but the innocent enjoy the story.' There is a truth represented for the imagination in these lines of a noble poem, where we are told, that in our highest hours of visionary clearness, we can but

'see the children sport upon the shoreAnd hear the mighty waters rolling evermore.'

To this clearness Fleeming had attained; and although he heard the voice of the eternal seas and weighed its message, he was yet able, until the end of his life, to sport upon these shores of death and mystery with the gaiety and innocence of children.

IV.

It was as a student that I first knew Fleeming, as one of that modest number of young men who sat under his ministrations in a soul-chilling class-room at the top of the University buildings. His presence was against him as a professor: no one, least of all students, would have been moved to respect him at first sight: rather short in stature, markedly plain, boyishly young in manner, cocking his head like a terrier with every mark of the most engaging vivacity and readiness to be pleased, full of words, full of paradox, a stranger could scarcely fail to look at him twice, a man thrown with him in a train could scarcely fail to be engaged by him in talk, but a student would never regard him as academical. Yet he had that fibre in him that order always existed in his class-room. I do not remember that he ever addressed me in language; at the least sign of unrest, his eye would fall on me and I was quelled. Such a feat is comparatively easy in a small class; but I have misbehaved in smaller classes and under eyes more Olympian than Fleeming Jenkin's. He was simply a man from whose reproof one shrank; in manner the least buckrammed of mankind, he had, in serious moments, an extreme dignity of goodness. So it was that he obtained a power over the most insubordinate of students, but a power of which I was myself unconscious. I was inclined to regard any professor as a joke, and Fleeming as a particularly good joke, perhaps the broadest in the vast pleasantry of my curriculum. I was not able to follow his lectures; I somehow dared not misconduct myself, as was my customary solace; and I refrained from attending. This brought me at the end of the session into a relation with my contemned professor that completely opened my eyes. During the year, bad student as I was, he had shown a certain leaning to my society; I had been to his house, he had asked me to take a humble part in his theatricals; I was a master in the art of extracting a certificate even at the cannon's mouth; and I was under no apprehension. But when I approached Fleeming, I found myself in another world; he would have naught of me. 'It is quite useless for YOU to come to me, Mr. Stevenson. There may be doubtful cases, there is no doubt about yours. You have simply NOT attended my class.' The document was necessary to me for family considerations; and presently I stooped to such pleadings and rose to such adjurations, as made my ears burn to remember. He was quite unmoved; he had no pity for me. - 'You are no fool,' said he, 'and you chose your course.' I showed him that he had misconceived his duty, that certificates were things of form, attendance a matter of taste. Two things, he replied, had been required for graduation, a certain competency proved in the final trials and a certain period of genuine training proved by certificate; if he did as I desired, not less than if he gave me hints for an examination, he was aiding me to steal a degree. 'You see, Mr. Stevenson, these are the laws and I am here to apply them,' said he. I could not say but that this view was tenable, though it was new to me; I changed my attack: it was only for my father's eye that I required his signature, it need never go to the Senatus, I had already certificates enough to justify my year's attendance. 'Bring them to me; I cannot take your word for that,' said he. 'Then I will consider.' The next day I came charged with my certificates, a humble assortment. And when he had satisfied himself, 'Remember,' said he, 'that I can promise nothing, but I will try to find a form of words.' He did find one, and I am still ashamed when I think of his shame in giving me that paper. He made no reproach in speech, but his manner was the more eloquent; it told me plainly what a dirty business we were on; and I went from his presence, with my certificate indeed in my possession, but with no answerable sense of triumph. That was the bitter beginning of my love for Fleeming; I never thought lightly of him afterwards.

Once, and once only, after our friendship was truly founded, did we come to a considerable difference. It was, by the rules of poor humanity, my fault and his. I had been led to dabble in society journalism; and this coming to his ears, he felt it like a disgrace upon himself. So far he was exactly in the right; but he was scarce happily inspired when he broached the subject at his own table and before guests who were strangers to me. It was the sort of error he was always ready to repent, but always certain to repeat; and on this occasion he spoke so freely that I soon made an excuse and left the house with the firm purpose of returning no more. About a month later, I met him at dinner at a common friend's. 'Now,' said he, on the stairs, 'I engage you - like a lady to dance - for the end of the evening. You have no right to quarrel with me and not give me a chance.' I have often said and thought that Fleeming had no tact; he belied the opinion then. I remember perfectly how, so soon as we could get together, he began his attack: 'You may have grounds of quarrel with me; you have none against Mrs. Jenkin; and before I say another word, I want you to promise you will come to HER house as usual.' An interview thus begun could have but one ending: if the quarrel were the fault of both, the merit of the reconciliation was entirely Fleeming's.

When our intimacy first began, coldly enough, accidentally enough on his part, he had still something of the Puritan, something of the inhuman narrowness of the good youth. It fell from him slowly, year by year, as he continued to ripen, and grow milder, and understand more generously the mingled characters of men. In the early days he once read me a bitter lecture; and I remember leaving his house in a fine spring afternoon, with the physical darkness of despair upon my eyesight. Long after he made me a formal retractation of the sermon and a formal apology for the pain he had inflicted; adding drolly, but truly, 'You see, at that time I was so much younger than you!' And yet even in those days there was much to learn from him; and above all his fine spirit of piety, bravely and trustfully accepting life, and his singular delight in the heroic.

His piety was, indeed, a thing of chief importance. His

views (as they are called) upon religious matters varied much; and he could never be induced to think them more or less than views. 'All dogma is to me mere form,' he wrote; 'dogmas are mere blind struggles to express the inexpressible. I cannot conceive that any single proposition whatever in religion is true in the scientific sense; and yet all the while I think the religious view of the world is the most true view. Try to separate from the mass of their statements that which is common to Socrates, Isaiah, David, St. Bernard, the Jansenists, Luther, Mahomet, Bunyan - yes, and George Eliot: of course you do not believe that this something could be written down in a set of propositions like Euclid, neither will you deny that there is something common and this something very valuable. . . . I shall be sorry if the boys ever give a moment's thought to the question of what community they belong to - I hope they will belong to the great community.' I should observe that as time went on his conformity to the church in which he was born grew more complete, and his views drew nearer the conventional. 'The longer I live, my dear Louis,' he wrote but a few months before his death, 'the more convinced I become of a direct care by God - which is reasonably impossible - but there it is.' And in his last year he took the communion.

But at the time when I fell under his influence, he stood more aloof; and this made him the more impressive to a youthful atheist. He had a keen sense of language and its imperial influence on men; language contained all the great and sound metaphysics, he was wont to say; and a word once made and generally understood, he thought a real victory of man and reason. But he never dreamed it could be accurate, knowing that words stand symbol for the indefinable. I came to him once with a problem which had puzzled me out of measure: what is a cause? why out of so many innumerable millions of conditions, all necessary, should one be singled out and ticketed 'the cause'? 'You do not understand,' said he. 'A cause is the answer to a question: it designates that condition which I happen to know and you happen not to know.' It was thus, with partial exception of the mathematical, that he thought of all means of reasoning: they were in his eyes but means of communication, so to be understood, so to be judged, and only so far to be credited. The mathematical he made, I say, exception of: number and measure he believed in to the extent of their significance, but that significance, he was never weary of reminding you, was slender to the verge of nonentity. Science was true, because it told us almost nothing. With a few abstractions it could deal, and deal correctly; conveying honestly faint truths. Apply its means to any concrete fact of life, and this high dialect of the wise became a childish jargon.

Thus the atheistic youth was met at every turn by a scepticism more complete than his own, so that the very weapons of the fight were changed in his grasp to swords of paper. Certainly the church is not right, he would argue, but certainly not the anti-church either. Men are not such fools as to be wholly in the wrong, nor yet are they so placed as to be ever wholly in the right. Somewhere, in mid air between the disputants, like hovering Victory in some design of a Greek battle, the truth hangs undiscerned. And in the meanwhile what matter these uncertainties? Right is very obvious; a great consent of the best of mankind, a loud voice within us (whether of God, or whether by inheritance, and in that case still from God), guide and command us in the path of duty. He saw life very simple; he did not love refinements; he was a friend to much conformity in unessentials. For (he would argue) it is in this life as it stands about us, that we are given our problem; the manners of the day are the colours of our palette; they condition, they constrain us; and a man must be very sure he is in the right, must (in a favourite phrase of his) be 'either very wise or very vain,' to break with any general consent in ethics. I remember taking his advice upon some point of conduct. 'Now,' he said, 'how do you suppose Christ would have advised you?' and when I had answered that he would not have counselled me anything unkind or cowardly, 'No,' he said, with one of his shrewd strokes at the weakness of his hearer, 'nor anything amusing.' Later in life, he made less certain in the field of ethics. 'The old story of the knowledge of good and evil is a very true one,' I find him writing; only (he goes on) 'the effect of the original dose is much worn out, leaving Adam's descendants with the knowledge that there is such a thing - but uncertain where.' His growing sense of this ambiguity made him less swift to condemn, but no less stimulating in counsel. 'You grant yourself certain freedoms. Very well,' he would say, 'I want to see you pay for them some other way. You positively cannot do this: then there positively must be something else that you can do, and I want to see you find that out and do it.' Fleeming would never suffer you to think that you were living, if there were not, somewhere in your life, some touch of heroism, to do or to endure.

This was his rarest quality. Far on in middle age, when men begin to lie down with the bestial goddesses, Comfort and Respectability, the strings of his nature still sounded as high a note as a young man's. He loved the harsh voice of duty like a call to battle. He loved courage, enterprise, brave natures, a brave word, an ugly virtue; everything that lifts us above the table where we eat or the bed we sleep upon. This with no touch of the motive-monger or the ascetic. He loved his virtues to be practical, his heroes to be great eaters of beef; he loved the jovial Heracles, loved the astute Odysseus; not the Robespierres and Wesleys. A fine buoyant sense of life and of man's unequal character ran through all his thoughts. He could not tolerate the spirit of the pick-thank; being what we are, he wished us to see others with a generous eye of admiration, not with the smallness of the seeker after faults. If there shone anywhere a virtue, no matter how incongruously set, it was upon the virtue we must fix our eyes. I remember having found much entertainment in Voltaire's SAUL, and telling him what seemed to me the drollest touches. He heard me out, as usual when displeased, and then opened fire on me with red-hot shot. To belittle a noble story was easy; it was not literature, it was not art, it was not morality; there was no sustenance in such a form of jesting, there was (in his favourite phrase) 'no nitrogenous food' in such literature. And then he proceeded to show what a fine fellow David was; and what a hard knot he was in about Bathsheba, so that (the initial wrong committed) honour might well hesitate in the choice of conduct; and what owls those people were who marvelled because an Eastern tyrant had killed Uriah, instead of marvelling that he had not killed the prophet also. 'Now if Voltaire had helped me to feel that,' said he, 'I could have seen some fun in it.' He loved the comedy which shows a hero human, and yet leaves him a hero, and the laughter which does not lessen love.

It was this taste for what is fine in human-kind, that ruled his choice in books. These should all strike a high note, whether brave or tender, and smack of the open air. The noble and simple presentation of things noble and simple, that was the 'nitrogenous food' of which he spoke so much, which he sought so eagerly, enjoyed so royally. He wrote to an author, the first part of whose story he had seen with sympathy, hoping that it might continue in the same vein. 'That this may be so,' he wrote, 'I long with the longing of David for the water of Bethlehem. But no man need die for the water a poet can give, and all can drink it to the end of time, and their thirst be quenched and the pool never dry - and the thirst and the water are both blessed.' It was in the Greeks particularly that he found this blessed water; he loved 'a fresh air' which he found 'about the Greek things even in translations'; he loved their freedom from the mawkish and the rancid. The tale of David in the Bible, the ODYSSEY, Sophocles, AEschylus, Shakespeare, Scott; old Dumas in his chivalrous note; Dickens rather than Thackeray, and the TALE OF TWO CITIES out of Dickens: such were some of his preferences. To Ariosto and Boccaccio he was always faithful; BURNT NJAL was a late favourite; and he found at least a passing entertainment in the ARCADIA and the GRAND CYRUS. George Eliot he outgrew, finding her latterly only sawdust in the mouth; but her influence, while it lasted, was great, and must have gone some way to form his mind. He was easily set on edge, however, by didactic writing; and held that books should teach no other lesson but what 'real life would teach, were it as vividly presented.' Again, it was the thing made that took him, the drama in the book; to the book itself, to any merit of the making, he was long strangely blind. He would prefer the AGAMEMNON in the prose of Mr. Buckley, ay, to Keats. But he was his mother's son, learning to the last. He told me one day that literature was not a trade; that it was no craft; that the professed author was merely an amateur with a door-plate. 'Very well,' said I, 'the first time you get a proof, I will demonstrate that it is as much a trade as bricklaying, and that you do not know it.' By the very next post, a proof came. I opened it with fear; for he was indeed, as the reader will see by these volumes, a formidable amateur; always wrote brightly, because he always thought trenchantly; and sometimes wrote brilliantly, as the worst of whistlers may sometimes stumble on a perfect intonation. But it was all for the best in the interests of his education; and I was able, over that proof, to give him a quarter of an hour such as Fleeming loved both to give and to receive. His subsequent training passed out of my hands into those of our common friend, W. E. Henley. 'Henley and I,' he wrote, 'have fairly good times wigging one another for not doing better. I wig him because he won't try to write a real play, and he wigs me because I can't try to write English.' When I next saw him, he was full of his new acquisitions. 'And yet I have lost something too,' he said regretfully. 'Up to now Scott seemed to me quite perfect, he was all I wanted. Since I have been learning this confounded thing, I took up one of the novels, and a great deal of it is both careless and clumsy.'

V.

He spoke four languages with freedom, not even English with any marked propriety. What he uttered was not so much well said, as excellently acted: so we may hear every day the inexpressive language of a poorly-written drama assume character and colour in the hands of a good player. No man had more of the

VIS COMICA in private life; he played no character on the stage, as he could play himself among his friends. It was one of his special charms; now when the voice is silent and the face still, it makes it impossible to do justice to his power in conversation. He was a delightful companion to such as can bear bracing weather; not to the very vain; not to the owlishly wise, who cannot have their dogmas canvassed; not to the painfully refined, whose sentiments become articles of faith. The spirit in which he could write that he was 'much revived by having an opportunity of abusing Whistler to a knot of his special admirers,' is a spirit apt to be misconstrued. He was not a dogmatist, even about Whistler. 'The house is full of pretty things,' he wrote, when on a visit; 'but Mrs. -'s taste in pretty things has one very bad fault: it is not my taste.' And that was the true attitude of his mind; but these eternal differences it was his joy to thresh out and wrangle over by the hour. It was no wonder if he loved the Greeks; he was in many ways a Greek himself; he should have been a sophist and met Socrates; he would have loved Socrates, and done battle with him staunchly and manfully owned his defeat; and the dialogue, arranged by Plato, would have shown even in Plato's gallery. He seemed in talk aggressive, petulant, full of a singular energy; as vain you would have said as a peacock, until you trod on his toes, and then you saw that he was at least clear of all the sicklier elements of vanity. Soundly rang his laugh at any jest against himself. He wished to be taken, as he took others, for what was good in him without dissimulation of the evil, for what was wise in him without concealment of the childish. He hated a draped virtue, and despised a wit on its own defence. And he drew (if I may so express myself) a human and humorous portrait of himself with all his defects and qualities, as he thus enjoyed in talk the robust sports of the intelligence; giving and taking manfully, always without pretence, always with paradox, always with exuberant pleasure; speaking wisely of what he knew, foolishly of what he knew not; a teacher, a learner, but still combative; picking holes in what was said even to the length of captiousness, yet aware of all that was said rightly; jubilant in victory, delighted by defeat: a Greek sophist, a British schoolboy.

Among the legends of what was once a very pleasant spot, the old Savile Club, not then divorced from Savile Row, there are many memories of Fleeming. He was not popular at first, being known simply as 'the man who dines here and goes up to Scotland'; but he grew at last, I think, the most generally liked of all the members. To those who truly knew and loved him, who had tasted the real sweetness of his nature, Fleeming's porcupine ways had always been a matter of keen regret. They introduced him to their own friends with fear; sometimes recalled the step with mortification. It was not possible to look on with patience while a man so lovable thwarted love at every step. But the course of time and the ripening of his nature brought a cure. It was at the Savile that he first remarked a change; it soon spread beyond the walls of the club. Presently I find him writing: 'Will you kindly explain what has happened to me? All my life I have talked a good deal, with the almost unfailing result of making people sick of the sound of my tongue. It appeared to me that I had various things to say, and I had no malevolent feelings, but nevertheless the result was that expressed above. Well, lately some change has happened. If I talk to a person one day, they must have me the next. Faces light up when they see me. - "Ah, I say, come here," - "come and dine with me." It's the most preposterous thing I ever experienced. It is curiously pleasant. You have enjoyed it all your life, and therefore cannot conceive how bewildering a burst of it is for the first time at forty-nine.' And this late sunshine of popularity still further softened him. He was a bit of a porcupine to the last, still shedding darts; or rather he was to the end a bit of a schoolboy, and must still throw stones, but the essential toleration that underlay his disputatiousness, and the kindness that made of him a tender sicknurse and a generous helper, shone more conspicuously through. A new pleasure had come to him; and as with all sound natures, he was bettered by the pleasure.

I can best show Fleeming in this later stage by quoting from a vivid and interesting letter of M. Emile Trelat's. Here, admirably expressed, is how he appeared to a friend of another nation, whom he encountered only late in life. M. Trelat will pardon me if I correct, even before I quote him; but what the Frenchman supposed to flow from some particular bitterness against France, was only Fleeming's usual address. Had M. Trelat been Italian, Italy would have fared as ill; and yet Italy was Fleeming's favourite country.

Vous savez comment j'ai connu Fleeming Jenkin! C'etait en Mai 1878. Nous etions tous deux membres du jury de l'Exposition Universelle. On n'avait rien fait qui vaille a la premiere seance de notre classe, qui avait eu lieu le matin. Tout le monde avait parle et reparle pour ne rien dire. Cela durait depuis huit heures; il etait midi. Je demandai la parole pour une motion d'ordre, et je proposai que la seance fut levee a la condition que chaque membre francais, EMPORTAT a dejeuner un jure etranger. Jenkin applaudit. 'Je vous emimene dejeuner,' lui criai-je. 'Je veux bien.' . . . Nous partimes; en chemin nous vous rencontrions; il vous presente et nous allons dejeuner tous trois aupres du Trocadero.

Et, depuis ce temps, nous avons ete de vieux amis. Non seulement nous passions nos journees au jury, ou nous etions toujours ensemble, cote-a-cote. Mais nos habitudes s'etaient faites telles que, non contents de dejeuner en face l'un de l'autre, je le ramenais diner presque tous les jours chez moi. Cela dura une quinzaine: puis il fut rappele en Angleterre. Mais il revint, et nous fimes encore une bonne etape de vie intellectuelle, morale et philosophique. Je crois qu'il me rendait deja tout ce que j'eprouvais de sympathie et d'estime, et que je ne fus pas pour rien dans son retour a Paris.

Chose singuliere! nous nous etions attaches l'un a l'autre par les sous-entendus bien plus que par la matiere de nos conversations. A vrai dire, nous etions presque toujours en discussion; et il nous arrivait de nous rire au nez l'un et l'autre pendant des heures, tant nous nous etonnions reciproquement de la diversite de nos points de vue. Je le trouvais si Anglais, et il me trouvais si Francais! Il etait si franchement revolte de certaines choses qu'il voyait chez nous, et je comprenais si mal certaines choses qui se passaient chez vous! Rien de plus interessant que ces contacts qui etaient des contrastes, et que ces rencontres d'idees qui etaient des choses; rien de si attachant que les echappees de coeur ou d'esprit auxquelles ces petits conflits donnaient a tout moment cours. C'est dans ces conditions que, pendant son sejour a Paris en 1878, je conduisis un peu partout mon nouvel ami. Nous all*f*mes chez Madame Edmond Adam, ou il vit passer beaucoup d'hommes politiques avec lesquels il causa.

Mais c'est chez les ministres qu'il fut interesse. Le moment etait, d'ailleurs, curieux en France. Je me rappelle que, lorsque je le presentai au Ministre du Commerce, il fit cette spirituelle repartie: 'C'est la seconde fois que je viens en France sous la Republique. La premiere fois, c'etait en 1848, elle s'etait coiffee de travers: je suis bien heureux de saluer aujourd'hui votre excellence, quand elle a mis son chapeau droit.' Une fois je le menai voir couronner la Rosiere de Nanterre. Il y suivit les ceremonies civiles et religieuses; il y assista au banquet donne par le Maire; il y vit notre de Lesseps, auquel il porta un toast. Le soir, nous revinmes tard a Paris; il faisait chaud; nous etions un peu fatigues; nous entr*f*mes dans un des rares cafes encore ouverts. Il devint silencieux. - 'N'etes-vous pas content de votre journee?' lui dis-je. - 'O, si! mais je reflechis, et je me dis que vous etes un peuple gai - tous ces braves gens etaient gais aujourd'hui. C'est une vertu, la gaiete, et vous l'avez en France, cette vertu!' Il me disait cela melancoliquement; et c'etait la premiere fois que je lui entendais faire une louange adressee a la France. . . . Mais il ne faut pas que vous voyiez la une plainte de ma part. Je serais un ingrat si je me plaignais; car il me disait souvent: 'Quel bon Francais vous faites!' Et il m'aimait a cause de cela, quoiqu'il sembl*f*t n'ainier pas la France. C'etait la un trait de son originalite. Il est vrai qu'il s'en tirait en disant que je ne ressemblai pas a mes compatriotes, ce a quoi il ne connaissait rien! - Tout cela etait fort curieux; car, moi-meme, je l'aimais quoiqu'il en e–t a mon pays!

En 1879 il amena son fils Austin a Paris. J'attirai celui-ci. Il dejeunait avec moi deux fois par semaine. Je lui montrai ce qu'etait l'intimite francaise en le tutoyant paternellement. Cela reserra beaucoup nos liens d'intimite avec Jenkin. . . . Je fis inviter mon ami au congres de l'ASSOCIATION FRANCAISE POUR L'AVANCEMENT DES SCIENCES, qui se tenait a Rheims en 1880. Il y vint. J'eus le plaisir de lui donner la parole dans la section du genie civil et militaire, que je presidais. Il y fit une tres interessante communication, qui me montrait une fois de plus l'originalite de ses vaes et la s–rete de sa science. C'est a l'issue de ce congres que je passai lui faire visite a Rochefort, ou je le trouvai installe en famille et ou je presentai pour la premiere fois mes hommages a son eminente compagne. Je le vis la sous un jour nouveau et touchant pour moi. Madame Jenkin, qu'il entourait si galamment, et ses deux jeunes fils donnaient encore plus de relief a sa personne. J'emportai des quelques heures que je passai a cote de lui dans ce charmant paysage un souvenir emu.

J'etais alle en Angleterre en 1882 sans pouvoir gagner Edimbourg. J'y retournai en 1883 avec la commission d'assainissement de la ville de Paris, dont je faisais partie. Jenkin me rejoignit. Je le fis entendre par mes collegues; car il etait fondateur d'une societe de salubrite. Il eut un grand succes parmi nous. Mais ce voyaye me restera toujours en memoire parce que c'est la que se fixa definitivement notre forte amitie. Il m'invita un jour a diner a son club et au moment de me faire asseoir a cote de lui, il me retint et me dit: 'Je voudrais vous demander de m'accorder quelque chose. C'est mon sentiment que nos relations ne peuvent pas se bien continuer si vous ne me donnez pas la permission de vous tutoyer. Voulez-vous que nous nous tutoyions?' Je lui pris les mains et je lui dis qu'une pareille proposition venant d'un Anglais, et d'un Anglais de sa haute distinction, c'etait une victoire, dont je serais fier toute ma vie. Et nous commencions a user de cette nouvelle forme dans nos rapports. Vous savez avec quelle finesse il parlait le francais: comme il en connaissait tous les tours, comme il jouait avec ses difficultes, et meme avec ses petites gamineries. Je crois qu'il a ete heureux de pratiquer avec moi ce tutoiement, qui ne s'adapte pas a l'anglais, et qui est si francais. Je ne puis vous peindre l'etendue et la variete de nos conversations de la soiree. Mais ce que je puis vous dire, c'est que, sous la caresse du TU, nos idees se sont elevees. Nous avions toujours beaucoup ri ensemble; mais nous n'avions jamais laisse des banalites s'introduire dans nos echanges de pensees. Ce soir-la, notre horizon intellectual s'est elargie, et nous y avons pousse des reconnaissances profondes et lointaines. Apres avoir vivement cause a table, nous avons longuement cause au salon; et nous nous separions le soir a Trafalgar Square, apres avoir longe les trotters, stationne aux coins des rues et deux fois rebrousse chemie en nous reconduisant l'un l'autre. Il etait pres d'une heure du matin! Mais quelle belle passe d'argumentation, quels beaux echanges de sentiments, quelles fortes confidences patriotiques nous avions fournies! J'ai compris ce soir la que Jenkin ne detestait pas la France, et je lui serrai fort les mains en l'embrassant. Nous nous quittions aussi amis qu'on puisse l'etre; et notre affection s'etait par lui etendue et comprise dans un TU francais.

CHAPTER VII. 1875-1885.

Mr Jenkin's Illness - Captain Jenkin - The Golden Wedding - Death of Uncle John - Death of Mr. and Mrs. Austin - Illness and Death of the Captain - Death of Mrs. Jenkin - Effect on Fleeming - Telpherage - The End.

AND now I must resume my narrative for that melancholy business that concludes all human histories. In January of the year 1875, while Fleeming's sky was still unclouded, he was reading Smiles. 'I read my engineers' lives steadily,' he writes, 'but find biographies depressing. I suspect one reason to be that misfortunes and trials can be graphically described, but happiness and the causes of happiness either cannot be or are not. A grand new branch of literature opens to my view: a drama in which people begin in a poor way and end, after getting gradually happier, in an ecstasy of enjoyment. The common novel is not the thing at all. It gives struggle followed by relief. I want each act to close on a new and triumphant happiness, which has been steadily growing all the while. This is the real antithesis of tragedy, where things get blacker and blacker and end in hopeless woe. Smiles has not grasped my grand idea, and only shows a bitter struggle followed by a little respite before death. Some feeble critic might say my new idea was not true to nature. I'm sick of this old-fashioned notion of art. Hold a mirror up, indeed! Let's paint a picture of how things ought to be and hold that up to nature, and perhaps the poor old woman may repent and mend her ways.' The 'grand idea' might be possible in art; not even the ingenuity of nature could so round in the actual life of any man. And yet it might almost seem to fancy that she had read the letter and taken the hint; for to Fleeming the cruelties of fate were strangely blended with tenderness, and when death came, it came harshly to others, to him not unkindly.

In the autumn of that same year 1875, Fleeming's father and mother were walking in the garden of their house at Merchiston, when the latter fell to the ground. It was thought at the time to be a stumble; it was in all likelihood a premonitory stroke of palsy. From that day, there fell upon her an abiding panic fear; that glib, superficial part of us that speaks and reasons could allege no cause, science itself could find no mark of danger, a son's solicitude was laid at rest; but the eyes of the body saw the approach of a blow, and the consciousness of the body trembled at its coming. It came in a moment; the brilliant, spirited old lady leapt from her bed, raving. For about six months, this stage of her disease continued with many painful and many pathetic circumstances; her husband who tended her, her son who was unwearied in his visits, looked for no change in her condition but the change that comes to all. 'Poor mother,' I find Fleeming writing, 'I cannot get the tones of her voice out of my head. . . I may have to bear this pain for a long time; and so I am bearing it and sparing myself whatever pain seems useless. Mercifully I do sleep, I am so weary that I must sleep.' And again later: 'I could do very well, if my mind did not revert to my poor mother's state whenever I stop attending to matters immediately before me.'

And the next day: 'I can never feel a moment's pleasure without having my mother's suffering recalled by the very feeling of happiness. A pretty, young face recalls hers by contrast - a careworn face recalls it by association. I tell you, for I can speak to no one else; but do not suppose that I wilfully let my mind dwell on sorrow.'

In the summer of the next year, the frenzy left her; it left her stone deaf and almost entirely aphasic, but with some remains of her old sense and courage. Stoutly she set to work with dictionaries, to recover her lost tongues; and had already made notable progress, when a third stroke scattered her acquisitions. Thenceforth, for nearly ten years, stroke followed upon stroke, each still further jumbling the threads of her intelligence, but by degrees so gradual and with such partiality of loss and of survival, that her precise state was always and to the end a matter of dispute. She still remembered her friends; she still loved to learn news of them upon the slate; she still read and marked the list of the subscription library; she still took an interest in the choice of a play for the theatricals, and could remember and find parallel passages; but alongside of these surviving powers, were lapses as remarkable, she misbehaved like a child, and a servant had to sit with her at table. To see her so sitting, speaking with the tones of a deaf mute not always to the purpose, and to remember what she had been, was a moving appeal to all who knew her. Such was the pathos of these two old people in their affliction, that even the reserve of cities was melted and the neighbours vied in sympathy and kindness. Where so many were more than usually helpful, it is hard to draw distinctions; but I am directed and I delight to mention in particular the good Dr. Joseph Bell, Mr. Thomas, and Mr. Archibald

Constable with both their wives, the Rev. Mr. Belcombe (of whose good heart and taste I do not hear for the first time - the news had come to me by way of the Infirmary), and their next-door neighbour, unwearied in service, Miss Hannah Mayne. Nor should I omit to mention that John Ruffini continued to write to Mrs. Jenkin till his own death, and the clever lady known to the world as Vernon Lee until the end: a touching, a becoming attention to what was only the wreck and survival of their brilliant friend.

But he to whom this affliction brought the greatest change was the Captain himself. What was bitter in his lot, he bore with unshaken courage; only once, in these ten years of trial, has Mrs. Fleeming Jenkin seen him weep; for the rest of the time his wife - his commanding officer, now become his trying child - was served not with patience alone, but with a lovely happiness of temper. He had belonged all his life to the ancient, formal, speechmaking, compliment-presenting school of courtesy; the dictates of this code partook in his eyes of the nature of a duty; and he must now be courteous for two. Partly from a happy illusion, partly in a tender fraud, he kept his wife before the world as a still active partner. When he paid a call, he would have her write 'with love' upon a card; or if that (at the moment) was too much, he would go armed with a bouquet and present it in her name. He even wrote letters for her to copy and sign: an innocent substitution, which may have caused surprise to Ruffini or to Vernon Lee, if they ever received, in the hand of Mrs. Jenkin the very obvious reflections of her husband. He had always adored this wife whom he now tended and sought to represent in correspondence: it was now, if not before, her turn to repay the compliment; mind enough was left her to perceive his unwearied kindness; and as her moral qualities seemed to survive quite unimpaired, a childish love and gratitude were his reward. She would interrupt a conversation to cross the room and kiss him. If she grew excited (as she did too often) it was his habit to come behind her chair and pat her shoulder; and then she would turn round, and clasp his hand in hers, and look from him to her visitor with a face of pride and love; and it was at such moments only that the light of humanity revived in her eyes. It was hard for any stranger, it was impossible for any that loved them, to behold these mute scenes, to recall the past, and not to weep. But to the Captain, I think it was all happiness. After these so long years, he had found his wife again; perhaps kinder than ever before; perhaps now on a more equal footing; certainly, to his eyes, still beautiful. And the call made on his intelligence had not been made in vain. The merchants of Aux Cayes, who had seen him tried in some 'counter-revolution' in 1845, wrote to the consul of his 'able and decided measures,' 'his cool, steady judgment and discernment' with admiration; and of himself, as 'a credit and an ornament to H. M. Naval Service.' It is plain he must have sunk in all his powers, during the years when he was only a figure, and often a dumb figure, in his wife's drawing-room; but with this new term of service, he brightened visibly. He showed tact and even invention in managing his wife, guiding or restraining her by the touch, holding family worship so arranged that she could follow and take part in it. He took (to the world's surprise) to reading - voyages, biographies, Blair's SERMONS, even (for her letter's sake) a work of Vernon Lee's, which proved, however, more than he was quite prepared for. He shone more, in his remarkable way, in society; and twice he had a little holiday to Glenmorven, where, as may be fancied, he was the delight of the Highlanders. One of his last pleasures was to arrange his dining-room. Many and many a room (in their wandering and thriftless existence) had he seen his wife furnish with exquisite taste, and perhaps with 'considerable luxury': now it was his turn to be the decorator. On the wall he had an engraving of Lord Rodney's action, showing the PROTHEE, his father's ship, if the reader recollects; on either side of this on brackets, his father's sword, and his father's telescope, a gift from Admiral Buckner, who had used it himself during the engagement; higher yet, the head of his grandson's first stag, portraits of his son and his son's wife, and a couple of old Windsor jugs from Mrs. Buckner's. But his simple trophy was not yet complete; a device had to be worked and framed and hung below the engraving; and for this he applied to his daughter-in-law: 'I want you to work me something, Annie. An anchor at each side - an anchor - stands for an old sailor, you know - stands for hope, you know - an anchor at each side, and in the middle THANKFUL.' It is not easy, on any system of punctuation, to represent the Captain's speech. Yet I hope there may shine out of these facts, even as there shone through his own troubled utterance, some of the charm of that delightful spirit.

In 1881, the time of the golden wedding came round for that sad and pretty household. It fell on a Good Friday, and its celebration can scarcely be recalled without both smiles and tears. The drawing-room was filled with presents and beautiful bouquets; these, to Fleeming and his family, the golden bride and bridegroom displayed with unspeakable pride, she so painfully excited that the guests feared every moment to see her stricken afresh, he guiding and moderating her with his customary tact and understanding, and doing the honours of the day with more than his usual delight. Thence they were brought to the dining-room, where the Captain's idea of a feast awaited them: tea and champagne, fruit and toast and childish little luxuries, set forth pell-mell and pressed at random on the guests. And here he must make a speech for himself and his wife, praising their destiny, their marriage, their son, their daughter-in-law, their grandchildren, their manifold causes of gratitude: surely the most innocent speech, the old, sharp contemner of his innocence now watching him with eyes of admiration. Then it was time for the guests to depart; and they went away, bathed, even to the youngest child, in tears of inseparable sorrow and gladness, and leaving the golden bride and bridegroom to their own society and that of the hired nurse.

It was a great thing for Fleeming to make, even thus late, the acquaintance of his father; but the harrowing pathos of such scenes consumed him. In a life of tense intellectual effort, a certain smoothness of emotional tenor were to be desired; or we burn the candle at both ends. Dr. Bell perceived the evil that was being done; he pressed Mrs. Jenkin to restrain her husband from too frequent visits; but here was one of those clear-cut, indubitable duties for which Fleeming lived, and he could not pardon even the suggestion of neglect.

And now, after death had so long visibly but still innocuously hovered above the family, it began at last to strike and its blows fell thick and heavy. The first to go was uncle John Jenkin, taken at last from his Mexican dwelling and the lost tribes of Israel; and nothing in this remarkable old gentleman's life, became him like the leaving of it. His sterling, jovial acquiescence in man's destiny was a delight to

Fleeming. 'My visit to Stowting has been a very strange but not at all a painful one,' he wrote. 'In case you ever wish to make a person die as he ought to die in a novel,' he said to me, 'I must tell you all about my old uncle.' He was to see a nearer instance before long; for this family of Jenkin, if they were not very aptly fitted to live, had the art of manly dying. Uncle John was but an outsider after all; he had dropped out of hail of his nephew's way of life and station in society, and was more like some shrewd, old, humble friend who should have kept a lodge; yet he led the procession of becoming deaths, and began in the mind of Fleeming that train of tender and grateful thought, which was like a preparation for his own. Already I find him writing in the plural of 'these impending deaths'; already I find him in quest of consolation. 'There is little pain in store for these wayfarers,' he wrote, 'and we have hope - more than hope, trust.'

On May 19, 1884, Mr. Austin was taken. He was seventy-eight years of age, suffered sharply with all his old firmness, and died happy in the knowledge that he had left his wife well cared for. This had always been a bosom concern; for the Barrons were long-lived and he believed that she would long survive him. But their union had been so full and quiet that Mrs. Austin languished under the separation. In their last years, they would sit all evening in their own drawing-room hand in hand: two old people who, for all their fundamental differences, had yet grown together and become all the world in each other's eyes and hearts; and it was felt to be a kind release, when eight months after, on January 14, 1885, Eliza Barron followed Alfred Austin. 'I wish I could save you from all pain,' wrote Fleeming six days later to his sorrowing wife, 'I would if I could - but my way is not God's way; and of this be assured, - God's way is best.'

In the end of the same month, Captain Jenkin caught cold and was confined to bed. He was so unchanged in spirit that at first there seemed no ground of fear; but his great age began to tell, and presently it was plain he had a summons. The charm of his sailor's cheerfulness and ancient courtesy, as he lay dying, is not to be described. There he lay, singing his old sea songs; watching the poultry from the window with a child's delight; scribbling on the slate little messages to his wife, who lay bed-ridden in another room; glad to have Psalms read aloud to him, if they were of a pious strain - checking, with an 'I don't think we need read that, my dear,' any that were gloomy or bloody. Fleeming's wife coming to the house and asking one of the nurses for news of Mrs. Jenkin, 'Madam, I do not know,' said the nurse; 'for I am really so carried away by the Captain that I can think of nothing else.' One of the last messages scribbled to his wife and sent her with a glass of the champagne that had been ordered for himself, ran, in his most finished vein of childish madrigal: 'The Captain bows to you, my love, across the table.' When the end was near and it was thought best that Fleeming should no longer go home but sleep at Merchiston, he broke his news to the Captain with some trepidation, knowing that it carried sentence of death. 'Charming, charming - charming arrangement,' was the Captain's only commentary. It was the proper thing for a dying man, of Captain Jenkin's school of manners, to make some expression of his spiritual state; nor did he neglect the observance. With his usual abruptness, 'Fleeming,' said he, 'I suppose you and I feel about all this as two Christian gentlemen should.' A last pleasure was secured for him. He had been waiting with painful interest for news of Gordon and

Khartoum; and by great good fortune, a false report reached him that the city was relieved, and the men of Sussex (his old neighbours) had been the first to enter. He sat up in bed and gave three cheers for the Sussex regiment. The subsequent correction, if it came in time, was prudently withheld from the dying man. An hour before midnight on the fifth of February, he passed away: aged eighty-four.

Word of his death was kept from Mrs. Jenkin; and she survived him no more than nine and forty hours. On the day before her death, she received a letter from her old friend Miss Bell of Manchester, knew the hand, kissed the envelope, and laid it on her heart; so that she too died upon a pleasure. Half an hour after midnight, on the eighth of February, she fell asleep: it is supposed in her seventy-eighth year.

Thus, in the space of less than ten months, the four seniors of this family were taken away; but taken with such features of opportunity in time or pleasant courage in the sufferer, that grief was tempered with a kind of admiration. The effect on Fleeming was profound. His pious optimism increased and became touched with something mystic and filial. 'The grave is not good, the approaches to it are terrible,' he had written in the beginning of his mother's illness: he thought so no more, when he had laid father and mother side by side at Stowting. He had always loved life; in the brief time that now remained to him, he seemed to be half in love with death. 'Grief is no duty,' he wrote to Miss Bell; 'it was all too beautiful for grief,' he said to me; but the emotion, call it by what name we please, shook him to his depths; his wife thought he would have broken his heart when he must demolish the Captain's trophy in the dining-room, and he seemed thenceforth scarcely the same man.

These last years were indeed years of an excessive demand upon his vitality; he was not only worn out with sorrow, he was worn out by hope. The singular invention to which he gave the name of telpherage, had of late consumed his time, overtaxed his strength and overheated his imagination. The words in which he first mentioned his discovery to me - 'I am simply Alnaschar' - were not only descriptive of his state of mind, they were in a sense prophetic; since whatever fortune may await his idea in the future, it was not his to see it bring forth fruit. Alnaschar he was indeed; beholding about him a world all changed, a world filled with telpherage wires; and seeing not only himself and family but all his friends enriched. It was his pleasure, when the company was floated, to endow those whom he liked with stock; one, at least, never knew that he was a possible rich man until the grave had closed over his stealthy benefactor. And however Fleeming chafed among material and business difficulties, this rainbow vision never faded; and he, like his father and his mother, may be said to have died upon a pleasure. But the strain told, and he knew that it was telling. 'I am becoming a fossil,' he had written five years before, as a kind of plea for a holiday visit to his beloved Italy. 'Take care! If I am Mr. Fossil, you will be Mrs. Fossil, and Jack will be Jack Fossil, and all the boys will be little fossils, and then we shall be a collection.' There was no fear more chimerical for Fleeming; years brought him no repose; he was as packed with energy, as fiery in hope, as at the first; weariness, to which he began to be no stranger, distressed, it did not quiet him. He feared for himself, not without ground, the fate which had overtaken his mother; others shared the fear. In the changed life now made for his family, the elders dead, the sons going from home upon their education, even their tried domestic (Mrs. Alice Dunns) leaving the house after twenty-two years of service, it was not unnatural that he should return to dreams of Italy. He and his wife were to go (as he told me) on 'a real honeymoon tour.' He had not been alone with his wife 'to speak of,' he added, since the birth of his children. But now he was to enjoy the society of her to whom he wrote, in these last days, that she was his 'Heaven on earth.' Now he was to revisit Italy, and see all the pictures and the buildings and the scenes that he admired so warmly, and lay aside for a time the irritations of his strenuous activity. Nor was this all. A trifling operation was to restore his former lightness of foot; and it was a renovated youth that was to set forth upon this re‰nacted honeymoon.

The operation was performed; it was of a trifling character, it seemed to go well, no fear was entertained; and his wife was reading aloud to him as he lay in bed, when she perceived him to wander in his mind. It is doubtful if he ever recovered a sure grasp upon the things of life; and he was still unconscious when he passed away, June the twelfth, 1885, in the fifty-third year of his age. He passed; but something in his gallant vitality had impressed itself upon his friends, and still impresses. Not from one or two only, but from many, I hear the same tale of how the imagination refuses to accept our loss and instinctively looks for his reappearing, and how memory retains his voice and image like things of yesterday. Others, the well-beloved too, die and are progressively forgotten; two years have passed since Fleeming was laid to rest beside his father, his mother, and his Uncle John; and the thought and the look of our friend still haunt us.

APPENDIX.

NOTE ON THE CONTRIBUTIONS OF FLEEMING JENKIN TO ELECTRICAL AND ENGINEERING SCIENCE. BY SIR WILLIAM THOMSON, F.R.S., LL D., ETC., ETC.

IN the beginning of the year 1859 my former colleague (the first British University Professor of Engineering), Lewis Gordon, at that time deeply engaged in the then new work of cable making and cable laying, came to Glasgow to see apparatus for testing submarine cables and signalling through them, which I had been preparing for practical use on the first Atlantic cable, and which had actually done service upon it, during the six weeks of its successful working between Valencia and Newfoundland. As soon as he had seen something of what I had in hand, he said to me, 'I would like to show this to a young man of remarkable ability, at present engaged in our works at Birkenhead.' Fleeming Jenkin was accordingly telegraphed for, and appeared next morning in Glasgow. He remained for a week, spending the whole day in my class-room and laboratory, and thus pleasantly began our lifelong acquaintance. I was much struck, not only with his brightness and ability, but with his resolution to understand everything spoken of, to see if possible thoroughly through every difficult question, and (no if about this!) to slur over nothing. I soon found that thoroughness of honesty was as strongly engrained in the scientific as in the moral side of his character.

In the first week of our acquaintance, the electric telegraph and, particularly, submarine cables, and the methods, machines, and instruments for laying, testing, and using them, formed naturally the chief subject of our conversations and discussions; as it was in fact the practical object of Jenkin's visit to me in Glasgow; but not much of the week had passed before I found him remarkably interested in science generally, and full of intelligent eagerness on many particular questions of dynamics and physics. When he returned from Glasgow to Birkenhead a correspondence commenced between us, which was continued without intermission up to the last days of his life. It commenced with a well-sustained fire of letters on each side about the physical qualities of submarine cables, and the practical results attainable in the way of rapid signalling through them. Jenkin used excellently the valuable opportunities for experiment allowed him by Newall, and his partner Lewis Gordon, at their Birkenhead factory. Thus he began definite scientific investigation of the copper resistance of the conductor, and the insulating resistance and specific inductive capacity of its gutta-percha coating, in the factory, in various stages of manufacture; and he was the very first to introduce systematically into practice the grand system of absolute measurement founded in Germany by Gauss and Weber. The immense value of this step, if only in respect to the electric telegraph, is amply appreciated by all who remember or who have read something of the history of submarine telegraphy; but it can scarcely be known generally how much it is due to Jenkin.

Looking to the article 'Telegraph (Electric)' in the last

volume of the old edition of the 'Encyclopaedia Britannica,' which was published about the year 1861, we find on record that Jenkin's measurements in absolute units of the specific resistance of pure gutta-percha, and of the gutta-percha with Chatterton's compound constituting the insulation of the Red Sea cable of 1859, are given as the only results in the way of absolute measurements of the electric resistance of an insulating material which had then been made. These remarks are prefaced in the 'Encyclopaedia' article by the following statement: 'No telegraphic testing ought in future to be accepted in any department of telegraphic business which has not this definite character; although it is only within the last year that convenient instruments for working, in absolute measure, have been introduced at all, and the whole system of absolute measure is still almost unknown to practical electricians.'

A particular result of great importance in respect to testing is referred to as follows in the 'Encyclopaedia' article: 'The importance of having results thus stated in absolute measure is illustrated by the circumstance, that the writer has been able at once to compare them, in the manner stated in a preceding paragraph, with his own previous deductions from the testings of the Atlantic cable during its manufacture in 1857, and with Weber's measurements of the specific resistance of copper.' It has now become universally adapted - first of all in England; twenty-two years later by Germany, the country of its birth; and by France and Italy, and all the other countries of Europe and America - practically the whole scientific world - at the Electrical Congress in Paris in the years 1882 and 1884.

An important paper of thirty quarto pages published in

the 'Transactions of the Royal Society' for June 19, 1862, under the title 'Experimental Researches on the Transmission of Electric Signals through submarine cables, Part I. Laws of Transmission through various lengths of one cable, by Fleeming Jenkin, Esq., communicated by C. Wheatstone, Esq., F.R.S.,' contains an account of a large part of Jenkin's experimental work in the Birkenhead factory during the years 1859 and 1860. This paper is called Part I. Part II. alas never appeared, but something that it would have included we can see from the following ominous statement which I find near the end of Part I.: 'From this value, the electrostatical capacity per unit of length and the specific inductive capacity of the dielectric, could be determined. These points will, however, be more fully treated of in the second part of this paper.' Jenkin had in fact made a determination at Birkenhead of the specific inductive capacity of gutta-percha, or of the gutta-percha and Chatterton's compound constituting the insulation of the cable, on which he experimented. This was the very first true measurement of the specific inductive capacity of a dielectric which had been made after the discovery by Faraday of the existence of the property, and his primitive measurement of it for the three substances, glass, shellac, and sulphur; and at the time when Jenkin made his measurements the existence of specific inductive capacity was either unknown, or ignored, or denied, by almost all the scientific authorities of the day.

The original determination of the microfarad, brought out under the auspices of the British Association Committee on Electrical Standards, is due to experimental work by Jenkin, described in a paper, 'Experiments on Capacity,' constituting No. IV. of the appendix to the Report presented by the Committee to the Dundee Meeting of 1867. No other determination, so far as I know, of this important element of electric measurement has hitherto been made; and it is no small thing to be proud of in respect to Jenkin's fame as a scientific and practical electrician that the microfarad which we now all use is his.

The British Association unit of electrical resistance, on which was founded the first practical approximation to absolute measurement on the system of Gauss and Weber, was largely due to Jenkin's zeal as one of the originators, and persevering energy as a working member, of the first Electrical Standards Committee. The experimental work of first making practical standards, founded on the absolute system, which led to the unit now known as the British Association ohm, was chiefly performed by Clerk Maxwell and Jenkin. The realisation of the great practical benefit which has resulted from the experimental and scientific work of the Committee is certainly in a large measure due to Jenkin's zeal and perseverance as secretary, and as editor of the volume of Collected Reports of the work of the Committee, which extended over eight years, from 1861 till 1869. The volume of Reports included Jenkin's Cantor Lectures of January, 1866, 'On Submarine Telegraphy,' through which the practical applications of the scientific principles for which he had worked so devotedly for eight years became part of general knowledge in the engineering profession.

Jenkin's scientific activity continued without abatement to the end. For the last two years of his life he was much occupied with a new mode of electric locomotion, a very remarkable invention of his own, to which he gave the name of 'Telpherage.' He persevered with endless ingenuity in carrying out the numerous and difficult mechanical arrangements essential to the project, up to the very last days of his work in life. He had completed almost every detail of the realisation of the system which was recently opened for practical working at Glynde, in Sussex, four months after his death.

His book on 'Magnetism and Electricity,' published as one of Longman's elementary series in 1873, marked a new departure in the exposition of electricity, as the first text-book containing a systematic application of the quantitative methods inaugurated by the British Association Committee on Electrical Standards. In 1883 the seventh edition was published, after there had already appeared two foreign editions, one in Italian and the other in German.

His papers on purely engineering subjects, though not numerous, are interesting and valuable. Amongst these may be mentioned the article 'Bridges,' written by him for the ninth edition of the 'Encyclopaedia Britannica,' and afterwards republished as a separate treatise in 1876; and a paper 'On the Practical Application of Reciprocal Figures to the Calculation of Strains in Framework,' read before the Royal Society of Edinburgh, and published in the 'Transactions' of that Society in 1869. But perhaps the most important of all is his paper 'On the Application of Graphic Methods to the Determination of the Efficiency of Machinery,' read before the Royal Society of Edinburgh, and published in the 'Transactions,' vol. xxviii. (1876-78), for which he was awarded the Keith Gold Medal. This paper was a continuation of the subject treated in 'Reulaux's Mechanism,' and, recognising the value of that work, supplied the elements required to constitute from Reulaux's kinematic system a full machine receiving energy and doing work.

www.ingramcontent.com/pod-product-compliance
Lightning Source LLC
Chambersburg PA
CBHW022358040426
42450CB00005B/238